BAWA
the Sri Lanka gardens

Text by David Robson
With photographs by Dominic Sansoni

With 303 illustrations, 235 in colour

This book is dedicated to the memories of Bevis and Geoffrey Bawa
and celebrates the two tropical gardens which they created on either side of the Bentota River

Acknowledgments

The authors wish to give special thanks to Dooland de Silva, the guardian and owner of Brief; to the members of the Lunuganga Trust – Sunethra Bandaranaike, Ward Beling, Channa Daswatte, Eugenie Mack and Suhanya Raffel, and its secretary, Janet Kanangeswaren; and to the guardians of Lunuganga, Michael Daniels and Asha de Silva.

They would also like to acknowledge the help received from many people, including C. Anjalendran, Michael Charnaud, Cedric de Silva, Palinda da Silva, S.M.A. Hameed, Ismeth Raheem, Barbara Sansoni, Laki Senanayake and Yanik Tissera.

Thanks are also due to the National Library of Australia and the Art Gallery of New South Wales for giving access to material relating to Donald Friend, and to Tea Trails Ltd and Jetwing Travel for granting permission to photograph their tea-estate bungalows and gardens. Thanks also to Cat Glover who provided editorial support and Sarah Praill who designed the layouts.

Picture credits (all photographs © Dominic Sansoni)

Front cover: Around the 'Bimpol' Stairs and Circular Pond, Brief

Back cover, clockwise from top: The Sundial in the Black Pavilion Pool, Lunuganga; Geoffrey Bawa in 1992; One of twin statues on the North Terrace of Lunuganga.

Page 1: The frangipani avenue seen across the Water Gardens, Lunuganga

Pages 2–3: The circular pond at the foot of the Bimpol Stairs, Brief

Pages 6–7: Detail from the mural painted in 1958 by Donald Friend on the entrance verandah at Brief

First published in the United Kingdom in 2008 by
Thames & Hudson Ltd, 181A High Holborn, London WC1V 7QX

First paperback edition 2017
Reprinted 2024

Bawa: The Sri Lanka Gardens © 2008
David Robson and Dominic Sansoni

All Rights Reserved. No part of this publication may be reproduced or transmitted in any form or by any means, electronic or mechanical, including photocopy, recording or any other information storage and retrieval system, without prior permission in writing from the publisher.

British Library Cataloguing-in-Publication Data
A catalogue record for this book is available from the British Library

ISBN 978-0-500-29292-1

Printed and bound in China by Toppan Leefung Printing Limited

Be the first to know about our new releases, exclusive content and author events by visiting
thamesandhudson.com
thamesandhudsonusa.com
thamesandhudson.com.au

Contents

6 Introduction

I
8 Sri Lanka – The Larger Garden

II
32 Two Brothers

III
40 Brief

IV
92 Lunuganga

172 Visiting Brief and Lunuganga

174 Glossary

175 Bibliography and Credits

Introduction

This is a celebration of two remarkable gardens and of the two remarkable brothers who made them. Bevis and Geoffrey Bawa were Sri Lankan, the sons of a successful Moorish lawyer and his Burgher wife, and grew up in a leafy suburb of Colombo during the final years of the British Empire. Bevis, born in 1909, showed little interest in studying. In 1927 his newly widowed mother installed him on a rubber estate called Brief near Aluthgama in south-western Sri Lanka and pushed him towards a career as a planter. From the beginning, however, he sought to combine planting with life as a part-time soldier and served as equerry to five successive British governors. Inevitably this caused him to neglect his estate, though he later lavished huge amounts of time and effort on the gardens around his bungalow. As the estate shrank, so his gardens flourished. Bevis was also a bon viveur and a raconteur of some reputation. He had a wide circle of friends and attracted visitors from all over the world. During the years following Sri Lanka's independence, Brief became one of the most influential small gardens in Asia.

Geoffrey, ten years younger than Bevis, was expected to follow in his father's footsteps and take up law. In 1938 he was packed off to England to study, and in 1948 he returned to Sri Lanka a fully fledged but reluctant lawyer. Inspired by the gardens at Brief and determined to outdo his brother, Geoffrey bought an abandoned estate called Lunuganga on the far side of the Bentota River from Brief and set out to transform it into a landscaped garden. The project awakened his interest in architecture, and he returned to England for further studies, finally qualifying as an architect in 1957 at the age of thirty-eight. Geoffrey went on to become one of the most influential Asian architects of his day, but over the next forty years he still managed to devote all of his spare time and most of his spare money to the improvement of his garden. Lunuganga came to be regarded as one of the most important gardens of the late twentieth century.

Bevis died in 1992 and Geoffrey in 2003. Their gardens survive and are open to the public. The photographs of them in this book were taken by Dominic Sansoni, who through his various publications has done much to broadcast a strong and colourful image of his native land around the world. His parents were close friends of the Bawas, and he knew both brothers and their gardens from a very early age. Dooland de Silva, who was Bevis's secretary, recalls typing a letter to Dominic and asking Bevis how he wanted it to be addressed: 'Dear Dom' or 'Dear Dominic'? 'Just put "Dear Humbug"!' came the reply. Sansoni has revisited the gardens with his camera and has attempted to capture them in their various moods and to convey the essential spirit of each place.

David Robson has written the words. He is an architect who has had a long association with Sri Lanka and who was a friend of Geoffrey Bawa. He has published a comprehensive monograph on Geoffrey's life and work, as well as a companion volume assessing his legacy. Robson has tried to set Brief and Lunuganga in a historical and cultural context, hopefully contradicting the commonly held view that they belong simply to a European tradition of garden-making and inviting readers to connect them to Sri Lankan precedents. He argues that Brief can be seen as one of the last in a long line of estate gardens, while Lunuganga was inspired in part by the great Sri Lankan landscapes of the classical period.

I
Sri Lanka – The Larger Garden

'Lunuganga from the start was to be an extension of the surroundings – a garden within a larger garden.' GEOFFREY BAWA, 1990

FORTY MILES FROM PARADISE

Sri Lanka lies a few degrees to the north of the equator and, on the map, seems to hang like a teardrop from the tip of the Indian peninsula. It is a mango-shaped island measuring some 440 kilometres in length from Point Pedro in the north to Dondra Head in the south, and 230 kilometres across at its widest point. Its surface area of 65,000 square kilometres is similar to that of the Republic of Ireland, though it is completely dwarfed by neighbouring India.

India and Sri Lanka are separated by a narrow and barely navigable channel known as the Palk Strait but are almost connected by a slender chain of islands known as Adam's Bridge. This sense of being together and yet remaining apart has determined the relationship between the two countries throughout their histories and is recalled in the *Ramayana*, the famous Hindu epic which tells of the abduction of Rama's bride by Ravanna, king of Lanka, and her subsequent rescue by the monkey king Hanuman.

Sri Lanka lies at the centre of the Indian Ocean and acts as a hinge-point between the Arabian Sea and the Bay of Bengal. For countless centuries it hosted Arab dhows from the west and Chinese junks from the east and served as a major entrepôt on what is sometimes described as the 'Silk Road of the Sea'. It thus attracted travellers from the beginning of recorded history, and many of these left their impressions of its astonishing physical beauty, among them the Chinese monk Fa-Hsien in the fifth century, the Italian adventurer Marco Polo in the 1200s, the Moor Ibn Batuta in the fourteenth century, and Robert Knox, a British captive of the kings of Kandy, during the seventeenth century.

The topography of Sri Lanka is dominated by a knot of mountains which lie to the south-west of its centre. These rise up steeply from the coastal plains to a height of nearly 2,500 metres and interact with the monsoon winds to determine the island's distinctive climate. The north-east monsoon brings rain to the entire mountain region from November to February, while the weaker south-west monsoon rains on the south-western slopes from late April until September. As a result the south-western quadrant of the island remains persistently hot and humid, while the north and east are relatively dry for a large part of the year.

Sri Lanka's main rivers all originate in the central massif. The longest and biggest by far is the Mahaweli Ganga, or Great Sand River. This rises on Horton Plains as two separate streams which meet near Gampola. It then flows in a clockwise spiral around Kandy before tumbling eastwards towards the plain to proceed majestically northwards to its delta in Kodiyar Bay on the east coast near Trincomalee. The Kelani Ganga also rises on Horton Plains and runs on a close parallel course to the

'And from Seyllan to Paradise is a distance of forty Italian miles; so that it is said, the sound of the waters falling from the fountain of Paradise is heard there.'
MARIGNOLLI, papal envoy to the court of Kublai Khan, 1349

Opposite: Areca-nut palms at the edge of a rice paddy

Below from left: Adam's Peak; Ambewela; Menik Ganga; south-coast beaches

'What though the spicy breezes
Blow soft o'er Ceylon's isle,
Where every prospect pleases
And only man is vile.'

BISHOP REGINALD HEBER, 1827

Mahaweli for a distance of 25 kilometres before turning westwards and winding its way to the coast just to the north of Colombo.

Today much of Sri Lanka's landscape is either man-made or the indirect result of human intervention. But it is still possible to catch glimpses of indigenous vegetation: the cloud-forests of the Knuckles Mountains to the north-east of Kandy; the rhododendron glades of the Peak Wilderness near the holy mountain of Sri Pada; the tropical rainforests of the Sinharajah surviving in the switchback folds of hills between the mountains and the south-west coast; the lagoons and mangrove swamps of the littoral; the dry-zone jungles of the northern and eastern plains with their scattered rocky outcrops; the parched near-desert landscapes of the north-east coast; the inhospitable dunes of the northern islands.

WHERE EVERY PROSPECT PLEASES

Sri Lanka has a population of some twenty million. Three-quarters of these are Sinhalese and are said to be the descendants of Aryans who migrated from northern India during the sixth century BC. A little under a fifth are Tamils, descended either from Dravidian people who crossed the Palk Strait from South India during the first millennium BC or from indentured plantation workers brought from India by the British during the nineteenth century to work on the tea estates. The rest are mainly Moors who trace their ancestry back to Arab traders, and a diminishing number of Burghers – mixed-race descendents of European colonists. The Bawa brothers' paternal grandfather was a Moor from Galle called Ahamadu Bawa, while their maternal grandfather, Frederick Justus Schrader, was a Burgher descended from a German mercenary who went to Ceylon with the Dutch East India Company at the beginning of the 1700s.

The Sinhalese first settled in the broad river valleys that run between the central mountains and the north-west coast. There, over the centuries, they developed a sophisticated system of tank-fed irrigation which enabled them to harness the rainfall of both monsoons and to build up a highly successful agrarian economy based around rice cultivation. The first tanks were formed simply by throwing earth bunds across streams to store water from the rainy season. In time, however, bigger and bigger tanks were built and connected by a sophisticated system of canals. This made it possible to tap the rivers before they reached the plains, to divert water from one catchment area to another across tens of kilometres, and to shift monsoon rainwater into areas of rain shadow.

A typical Sinhalese village consisted of a straggle of simple straw-roofed wattle-and-daub huts strung out on higher ground above the rice

fields. A homestead might comprise a main pavilion with a covered verandah facing the village footpath and a collection of subsidiary structures including a kitchen and a rice bin which formed a more private rear space. The homestead would be surrounded by a vegetable garden and a plantation of fruit trees and shrubs. Land beyond the village was held in common and used for grazing animals, for growing timber-bearing trees and, in outlying areas, for slash-and-burn cultivation.

The Sinhalese established their capital, Anuradhapura, on the left bank of the Malwatu Oya at a point halfway between the mountains and the sea, and close to the main land route linking the ports of Mannar on the west coast and Trincomalee on the east coast. Anuradhapura presided over a millennium of relative peace and prosperity, and became one of the most magnificent cities of the ancient world. The central walled town was surrounded by an inner cordon of large Buddhist monasteries and an outer cordon of water tanks which supplied the townsfolk with water and irrigated their rice fields.

At the beginning of the eleventh century, invaders from South India sacked Anuradhapura. They ruled there for almost a century until they were expelled by Sinhalese forces from the southern kingdom of Ruhunu who then moved the capital further east to Polonnaruwa. After barely seven decades of peace and prosperity, Sri Lanka was again overrun by marauders from South India. The Sinhalese finally abandoned their traditional dry-zone lands and took refuge in the central mountains, thus distancing themselves from the northern Tamils. The great system of irrigation which at its peak had fed large swathes of the northern and eastern plains was abandoned: tank bunds were breached, canals silted up, and the jungles returned.

There followed a long period of instability during which two and sometimes even three separate kingdoms coexisted and the Sinhalese capital shifted from place to place, until it was finally established at the heart of the central highlands in Kandy. The ordinary folk adapted their earlier pattern of settlement to their new environment. Rainfall was abundant, and it was no longer necessary to store water in tanks. The valley floors were sculpted into gravity-fed rice terraces, and homesteads were located on the steep hillsides under a thick canopy of trees. Above the villages the hills belonged nominally to king or temple and were used for grazing or for shifting cultivation.

Meanwhile the coastal ports had developed as cosmopolitan centres, playing host to traders from China in the east and Arabia in the west. For a thousand years the ocean was dominated by Arabs who had mastered the art of sailing with the monsoons and established trading outposts

Above from left: Kelani Ganga; Rice fields in front of the Ritigala mountain. Below from left: Prawn traps in the lagoon at Balapitiya; mudding the rice

Opposite from top left: Rice, rubber, tea and eucalyptus near Castlereagh

around the edge of the Indian Ocean from Zanzibar to Java with important entrepôts on Sri Lanka's north-west coast. After 1500, however, European navies, attracted by the burgeoning spice trade, began to challenge Arab supremacy, and during the sixteenth century Portuguese colonists established control over Sri Lanka's coastal regions. In the mid-1600s the Portuguese were displaced by the Dutch, who in turn were displaced by the British.

The British extended their control over the interior and finally defeated the last of the Sinhalese kings in 1815. They were the first colonizers to exploit the natural resources of the island in a systematic way, and during the nineteenth century they cleared large areas to establish a plantation economy based on coconut, rubber and tea. To this end they developed the port of Colombo, which was connected to the rest of the island by a system of trunk roads and railways.

In 1948 Ceylon finally regained its independence after four centuries of foreign rule and became a Dominion within the British Commonwealth. The name 'Ceylon' was in fact the English version of a European concoction which had manifested itself as 'Ceilao' in Portuguese and 'Zeilan' in Dutch. When the island became a republic in 1972, it was renamed Sri Lanka, meaning the Resplendent Land.

Below: The elephant rock at the Isurumuniya Temple, Anuradhapura

Opposite from top: Boulders with drip ledges, Vessagiriya Monastery, Anuradhapura; Distant view of the Mirisawetiya Dagoba from the Vessagiriya ruins; The Anuradhapura Vessagiriya ruins themselves

A TWO-THOUSAND-YEAR TRADITION

Rocks and boulders have always featured as important elements in the Sri Lankan idea of landscape. The island's earliest inhabitants were hunter-gatherers who dwelt in caves or built shelters in and around clusters of boulders. For them the rocky landscape offered safety and protection but also harboured hidden dangers. They imbued stones and trees with animistic spirits, the forerunners of a panoply of deities who survive to this day in village dewales. The Sinhalese settlers who arrived during the early part of the first millennium BC began the process of civilizing the wilderness, of taming and personifying the demons. They avoided rocky terrain and settled in the broad, open river valleys. As the agrarian way of life took hold, the ancient caves and boulders were taken over by solitary shamans and meditating recluses. After the introduction of Buddhism during the third century BC, these were replaced by monks, and in time some caves became fully fledged monasteries in which a mixture of caves and conventional buildings interacted with trees, rocks and pools to create a unique contemplative landscape.

From earliest times, Sri Lankan architects have built with nature, treating the interventions of topography, vegetation and water as both constraints and opportunities. They have used materials gathered from sites and their surroundings – earth, stone and wood – to create buildings which interact in a deliberately symbiotic way with their natural settings. More formal buildings such as monasteries and palaces were invariably planned on rectangular grids aligned with the points of the compass. Strict symmetry, however, would always be broken in order to incorporate significant natural features, while levels would be adjusted so that the structures would run with the contours. Buildings were sited in relationship to each other so as to define clearly functional outdoor spaces; intermediate spaces such as loggias and courtyards were used to create buffer zones between interior and exterior.

Japanese Zen Buddhist garden design follows a number of guiding principles, one of which is known as *fukinsei*. This argues that asymmetry is fundamental to Buddhist thought; that imbalance is dynamic; that people should never strive to achieve perfection in what they make; that a garden is not static and so is never finished. There does not appear to have been any explicit formulation of such a principle in the Sri Lankan tradition, but the idea of *fukinsei* informs much of Sinhalese site planning and garden design. Designers invariably allowed nature to interrupt a formal arrangement and to break any obvious symmetries, seeking to achieve 'careful casualness' and to imbue their architecture with a picturesque quality.

Water has been a central component of Sri Lankan culture and consciousness since earliest times and is another key element of the landscape. The harvesting, conservation and distribution of water have played pivotal roles in the development of the economy and in the structuring of social institutions. One king even decreed that no single drop of water should reach the sea before it had passed through the bellies of at least six men or animals. But water is not simply regarded in a utilitarian way: it has also taken on spiritual, sensual and aesthetic dimensions. The evening congregation at a village tank reveals the extent to which the act of bathing has been ritualized: as the burning equatorial sun sinks below the horizon, people refresh themselves in the cooling waters, immersing themselves repeatedly and pouring scoops of water over their heads. To this day many urban Sri Lankans prefer to douse themselves with scoops of water rather than stand under a modern shower.

BOULDER GARDENS – VESSAGIRIYA, ISURUMUNIYA AND THE RANMASU-UYANA

The phrase 'boulder garden' was coined by the archaeologist Senake Bandaranayake in 1974 to describe a particular phenomenon of Sinhalese garden design: the incorporation of rocky outcrops

1 Sri Lanka – The Larger Garden

Below: Vessagiriya ruins, Anuradhapura

Opposite from top:
Isurumuniya; Ranmasu-uyana, Anuradhapura: the pools; Ranmasu-uyana: the royal bath

and areas of natural landscape into formal compositions of buildings. Boulder gardens came into their own during the first millennium AD and were associated with both monasteries and royal palaces. Some were wholly secular and associated with bathing and recreation, while others were given religious and ritualistic significance and used as places for contemplation. In either case, they expressed the deep attachment of the Sinhalese to their landscape and to water and the rituals of bathing.

A succession of boulder gardens can be seen below the bund of the Tissa Wewa reservoir in the south-western sector of Anuradhapura. The reservoir itself dates from 240 BC and represents a significant feat of hydraulic engineering. Covering an area of 200 hectares, it is fed by a canal that brings water a distance of 90 kilometres at minimal gradients from the Kala Wewa, feeding thirty-two intermediate tanks and serving more than a hundred villages along its route.

Running parallel with the reservoir's bund is a line of three groups of ruins which follow a broken ridge of scattered boulders: the rock-strewn monastery of Vessagiriya, the temple of the Isurumuniya, and the royal bathing pavilions of the Ranmasu-uyana. The whole composition symbolizes the epic struggle of the Sinhalese to civilize the wilderness of Sri Lanka and harness its water resources. The result is an aesthetic of landscaping architecture and garden design of enormous sophistication, a triumph of picturesque planning.

At the south end of the strip are the ruins of the 'organic monastery' known as the Vessagiriya. A low ridge of bare rock is studded with three separate clusters of free-standing boulders, some of them tens of metres high, many leaning at uncanny angles. Shelters for early Stone Age people, these were later inhabited by hermit monks and were finally integrated into a formally planned monastic complex during the fifth century AD. Time and vandals have stripped away most of the later buildings leaving an impressive assortment of caves and boulders with carved drip ledges, staircases and foundation sockets, as well the outlines of the formal buildings that once existed on the surrounding flat land.

A few hundred metres to the north lie the ruins of the Isurumuniya Temple, which in former times were contained within a moated precinct. The name means 'a place fit for ascetics'; the chronicles record that King Kasyapa, atoning for having murdered his father, restored the temple during the sixth century and 'planted gardens about the gates of the city and mango groves over the Island'. Today the site is dominated by a modern temple constructed within and around a clump of large boulders. But the site is much older, and the main image-cave was in use as early as the third century BC. The organic nature of the rock is expressed in a number of fluid carvings – one depicting a bathing elephant, another a man with his horse – which serve to highlight the contrast between buildings and boulders.

Further north still, the Royal Pleasure Gardens are set out along a north–south axis which runs parallel to the massive tank bund. Here the star attractions are two small stepped bathing pools inserted into a cluster of rocks, each with its own pavilion carved partly out of the living stone. Nearby three larger ornamental ponds survive among the bushes. The formality of the built elements contrasts with the liberal scattering of boulders incorporated into the composition. This is an early example of

Below: Pavilion in the ruins of the Abhayagiri Vihare, Anuradhapura

Opposite from left: Pavilion in the ruins of the Abhayagiri Vihare; The elephant bathing pool at Abhayagiri Vihare

a secular pleasure garden planned using the principles that had evolved in the design of monastic precincts. Situated immediately below the tank bund, the garden could draw on unlimited supplies of pressurized water and incorporated fountains and jets. The various water features were connected by a system of conduits and open rills. The chronicles suggest that this garden was liberally planted with flowering shrubs and ornamental trees.

These three ruins demonstrate how the Sinhalese attitude to the natural landscape evolved from utility to spirituality and, finally, to delight. At the Vessagiriya the existing boulders were first taken over as useful shelters, only later becoming the core of a formally planned monastic complex. At the Isurumuniya the boulders were selected for their spiritual and ritualistic meanings to form an integral part of a constructed temple building. In the Royal Pleasure Gardens the existing rock formations are incorporated into a picturesque composition following a consciously applied aesthetic system.

PARK MONASTERIES – THE ABHAYAGIRI VIHARE IN ANURADHAPURA

Today the whole of the ruined city of Anuradhapura reads as one huge park landscape, though it is still possible to identify the location of the original walled city and to distinguish the large monasteries which formed a loose cordon around it. The most impressive of these, the Abhayagiri Vihare, is located to the north-west of the citadel and has been described as a typical 'park monastery'. Park monasteries, or arama, were

planned in harmony with the natural elements of the landscape – rocky outcrops, boulders, caves, forest groves, trees, pools and streams – and developed as a complex interplay between formal architectural ideas and the informality of their settings.

The Abhayagiriya was founded during the first century BC and at its zenith housed more than five thousand monks in buildings which covered a site of 250 hectares. This vast complex was dominated by a gigantic stupa raised by King Gajabahu in the second century AD and second only in size to the Jetavanarama nearby. The stupa was surrounded by a number of more or less self-contained clusters, each comprising several monastic units. Such units were often laid out as quincunxes with five pavilions arranged symmetrically within a containing wall, the four peripheral ones functioning as dormitories with the central one housing the chief monk and serving as a place of prayer and study. Although the spatial and organizational hierarchies of these monasteries seem simple enough on plan, in reality the buildings interact with topography, landscape and water bodies to set up an ever-changing sequence of scales, containments, levels and vistas.

When we visit the monasteries of Anuradhapura and Polonnaruwa today, we see them very much as Bevis and Geoffrey Bawa would have seen them when they explored Ceylon during the 1950s, and we experience what the writer Rose Macaulay described as the 'Pleasure of Ruins'. We discover a wonderland of hauntingly beautiful but broken buildings which lay scattered across a wooded landscape, rising and falling with the contours, dodging the outcrops of rocks, embracing the pools and streams. And we admire what we see without fully understanding the significance of what it once might have been. But we can try to imagine narrow, shady alleyways running between raised brick walls, imposing porches opening onto sunlit courtyards of brushed sand, elegant pavilions raised up on carved stone plinths under geometrically tiled roofs, intricately carved moon-stones and guard-stones, exquisitely carved Buddha and bodhisattva figures, brilliant white stupas with golden spires, gurgling rills of water feeding stone-lined bathing ponds, groves of gently swaying trees, and everywhere clusters of massive boulders erupting out of the earth. And so we can begin to understand the subtlety and sophistication of the buildings and landscape planning created by Sinhalese architects.

Below: Kaludia Pokuna, Mihintale: the meditation rock

Opposite: Kaludia Pokuna, Mihintale: the library

KALUDIA POKUNA – THE BLACK POOL

The monastic remains of Mihintale lie some 16 kilometres east of Anuradhapura, nestling within a group of rock-strewn hills which rise steeply from the flat pastoral plain to a height of 300 metres. The ruins respond beautifully to the rugged topography to create an ever-changing scenography of boulder landscape and monument, and are revered as one of Sri Lanka's most important religious sites, marking the spot where, according to tradition, the missionary Thera Mahinda converted King Devanampiya-Tissa to Buddhism on the full-moon day of the month of Poson in 247 BC.

Most visitors are content simply to clamber up the monumental flights of stone steps between the lines of trees, planted by the archaeologist Senarat Paranavitana in the 1950s, and visit the monastic remains scattered among the various peaks. Few take the trouble to visit the Kaludia Pokuna, or Black Pool, a small reservoir surrounded by a ruined monastery that lies hidden a few minutes' walk away to the south, at the foot of the western slopes.

The pokuna is retained by a short bund spanning two groups of boulders, and its shape is determined by the topography of the surrounding hills. It served no practical agricultural purpose and must have been conceived as a place for ritual bathing as well as for cleansing and recreation. Visitors would have climbed a stone staircase that wound its way up the western face of the bund between the encompassing boulders to arrive at a reception kiosk affording a view of the whole complex. The view southwards from the kiosk across the pokuna is blocked by a remarkable trio of leaning boulders resembling a row of books, the top of which served as a meditation platform. The main monastic buildings were arranged along the axis of the bund on the western side of the pokuna. Here, buried below a group of boulders, is a cave with an elegant stone front which may have served as the monastery's library. Above it, perched bizarrely on the top of a large boulder, are two

square platforms separated by an artificial moat cut into the rock and connected by a stone bridge.

The more public parts of the monastery, which included a substantial dagoba, were situated just to the north of the entrance pavilion. The most striking feature, however, must have been the terrace built on an isolated rock projecting out into the north-eastern part of the pokuna. The rock's lower sides were encased in a massive retaining wall to create a flat terrace in the form of a prow, giving it the appearance of a large boat jutting out into the water, and it may well have functioned as a seema mallika, or ordination building.

The Kaludia Pokuna offers a graphic demonstration of the aesthetic principles that were applied by the architect monks of the later Anuradhapura period. All of the main enclosures were aligned to the points of the compass and organized within a complex system of symmetries and asymmetries. The apparent formalities of the planning were modified, however, by the existing topography, and the site was organized as a series of terraces. Today the Kaludia Pokuna is still home to a small community of ascetic monks who have established a meditational path and a cave dwelling below the bund. It is also visited by cormorants, herons, sea-eagles and brahminy kites and, in the late afternoon, by local villagers who use the rocks to wash their clothes before indulging in the time-honoured bathing rituals of the rural Sinhalese.

FOREST MONASTERIES – THE WESTERN MONASTERIES OF ANURADHAPURA AND THE RITIGALA FOREST MONASTERY

During the eighth century AD, a group of monks known as the Pamsukulikas, or Ragged Robed, broke away from the Mahavihare in Anuradhapura and established a cluster of monasteries on the western edge of the city. They were rebelling against what they saw as the excessive indulgences and rituals of the main monasteries and followed a life of austerity and asceticism. Their monasteries were built without image houses, stupas or bodhigaras and consisted of simple walled enclosures containing groups of pavilions built without adornment.

The Pamsukulikas also founded contemplative monasteries in remote forest areas, the best known being at Ritigala and Arankale. Ritigala is an isolated mountain situated halfway between Anuradhapura and Polonnaruwa which rises abruptly to a height of 600 metres above the surrounding plain and has a unique microclimate supporting an unexpected collection of montane flora. The monks settled on the heavily forested eastern slopes and lived in scattered caves and simple pavilions in an area criss-crossed by deep, rocky ravines. The backbone of their community was a string of formal buildings connected by an immaculate pavement of dressed stone which wound its way up between the ravines.

Ritigala today seems a place of magic and mystery. The peaks are often shrouded in cloud, and strange convection breezes waft clouds of butterflies through the ruins on the stillest of days. The seasonal torrents which crash down through the ravines have long since breached the Banda Pokuna's bund and tossed the stones to one side, while tree roots have shifted the foundations of the buildings and the ruins have been totally enveloped by the landscape.

Above: Western Monastery I, Anuradhapura: a 'bridge' between the raised platforms. Below from left: Western Monastery I, Anuradhapura: a 'moat' of bedrock separating two raised plinths; Ritigala: the approach stair; Ritigala: the stone pavement

Opposite: Aerial view of Sigiriya showing the Rock Citadel towering above the Royal Water Gardens

A ROYAL PLEASURE GARDEN

The great citadel rock of Sigiriya rears up some 200 metres above the boulder-scattered plains of central Sri Lanka at a point halfway between Anuradhapura and Polonnaruwa. Although the site was occupied from prehistoric times and was home to an extensive community of monks during the early Buddhist period, it was only during the latter part of the sixth century that it flourished as an important town and royal seat, for it was here that the usurper king Kasyapa, fearing retribution from his brother, established his stronghold. During his eighteen-year reign, according to the chronicles, he built an elaborate citadel palace on the summit of the rock and below it laid out a substantial town to the east and a huge water garden to the west.

Kasyapa's Royal Water Gardens were the greatest single achievement of Sinhalese landscape design and covered an area measuring about 600 metres from north to south and 450 metres from east to west, all contained within a double system of moats and ramparts. The main entrance to the gardens and, ultimately, to the palace citadel was from the west via a gateway and bridge set on axis in the western rampart. Visitors first entered the Charh Bagh, a large walled enclosure with gates on each axis containing a square pool divided into four quadrants with a square pavilion set on an island at its centre. This is one of the oldest surviving examples of what would later become a popular feature of South Asian gardens. The plan is rigidly symmetrical, but close inspection reveals that large outcrops of rock were allowed to break through the retaining walls and act as submarine features within the pools. Two tiny walled gardens, tucked away between the Charh Bagh and the western ramparts on either side of the main axis, have recently come to light. In contrast with the grand scale of the main garden, these had a refreshing intimacy and seem to have functioned as miniature spas, each with a complex arrangement of small water courts and bathing pavilions.

1 Sri Lanka – The Larger Garden

Above: Sigiriya Rock seen from the upper water garden

Opposite from top: Sigiriya: inside the Boulder Garden; Naked rock left exposed in the Charh Bagh; Staircases within the Boulder Garden

Beyond the Charh Bagh was the 'Fountain Court', a narrow walled garden, 150 metres in length, containing fountains and a serpentine rill. On either side there were two large moated pavilions, each built off bedrock and contained within an organically shaped pool. These formed a north–south axis and linked to a further pair of charh baghs at the northern and southern edges of the garden. The outer residual areas between the cross axes have yet to be investigated, but it seems possible that these may have contained planted gardens and orchards.

The fountain court led the visitor to a raised water-garden terrace with a large octagonal pond that preceded what is now called the 'Boulder Garden'. The piles of rocky debris at the foot of the cliff had long been home to hermit monks, but during Kasyapa's time the chaotic tumble of caves and boulders was transformed into a lower annex of the palace: a warren of structures incorporating offices, reception buildings and Buddhist shrines within a maze of narrow alleyways, steep stone staircases, small planted areas, fountain courts and watercourses. Above the Boulder Garden, a long walled gallery traversed the entire length of the base of the cliff face (below the famous Sigiriya wall paintings) and connected to the Lion Platform. From there a ceremonial flight of stairs climbed up to the summit between the paws of a monumental lion statue. This final ascent symbolized Kasyapa's position as king omnipotent of the Sinhalese – the 'lion people' – and master of Sigiriya – the 'lion rock'. The palace on the summit was an impressive affair, consisting of massive brick pavilions with courtyards, gardens and bathing ponds. All were aligned on the compass and fell with the contours, north to south and west to east, on a series of terraces, thus offering astonishing views across the plain in every direction.

Geoffrey Bawa's design for the Polontalawa Estate Bungalow (1964) was clearly inspired by the Sigiriya Boulder Garden, and in his first swimming pool at the Bentota Beach Hotel (1968) the rectangular basin was disrupted by an outcrop of rocks which recalled the Sigiriya Charh Bagh. Later he turned down an invitation to design a hotel at the foot of the Sigiriya rock, persuading his clients to shift their project to a rocky promontory overlooking the Kandalama Tank, some 8 kilometres to the south. There, inspired by Kasyapa's anonymous architects, he built a stunning hotel in the form of a palatial belvedere which focused on the distant view of the Sigiriya.

Above: Views of the Peradeniya Botanic Gardens

Opposite from top: An early estate bungalow in the midst of new jungle clearing; Spectators at an up-country cricket match; The Grand Hotel, Nuwara Eliya; An early tea-estate bungalow

THE PLANTATION RAJ

After the final collapse of the Polonnaruwa kingdom during the thirteenth century, the Sinhalese retreated southwards into the central highland area, where they established a much simpler system of rain-fed agriculture. There followed a period of uncertainty during which the capital shifted from place to place before finally settling in Maha Nuwara, which is present-day Kandy.

The Portuguese first arrived off the west coast in 1505, soon establishing a presence on the island. Their main aim was to control the lucrative trade in spices, and to that end they sought to dominate the ocean and control the major ports. In fact they were only able to control a thin strip of coastline and were content to manage the gathering of spices without getting directly involved with their production. When the Dutch ousted the Portuguese, they followed the latter's example, though during the final decades of Dutch presence the occupiers began to develop extensive coconut plantations and to experiment with the cultivation of cinnamon. The British displaced the Dutch in 1796 and, after a long campaign, succeeded in toppling the last king of Kandy in 1815, becoming the first foreign power to control the whole of Sri Lanka. While their presence was doubtless viewed as a mixed blessing by many, the period of their rule can be viewed as one of stability and economic progress, the first that Sri Lankans had experienced for seven centuries.

The British were not content to trade in spices; they were keen to involve themselves in the large-scale production of native plants and to experiment with the production of species from other parts of the world. For them Sri Lanka was a large garden, a garden waiting to be exploited, and during the 1800s they succeeded in transforming vast areas into profitable plantations.

For 150 years, Sri Lanka was part of the world's first global empire. The British during this time were responsible not only for shifting large numbers of people from continent to continent but also for redistributing flora and fauna on a massive scale. A key feature of this process was a system of botanic gardens which functioned like transit camps in a global plant-exchange system centred on the Royal Botanic Gardens at Kew.

Kew, a former royal park on the banks of the Thames near Richmond, was transformed into a major specimen garden during the reign of George III by the naturalist Joseph Banks. Banks had attained celebrity when he had travelled round the world on the first voyage of the *Endeavour* with Captain James Cook in 1768; later he was elected President of the Royal Society. A close adviser of the king, Banks dispatched botanists and explorers to many parts of the world to collect plants for Kew Gardens and was responsible for the setting up of a number of satellite botanic gardens in the colonies.

It was Banks who directed in 1810 that the first botanic garden be established in Sri Lanka. A former Dutch herbarium in Slave Island, an area of dry land surrounded by swamps to the immediate south of the Colombo Fort, was set aside for the purpose. The aims were twofold: to collect Sri Lankan plants for dispatch back to the central garden in Britain and thence to other parts of the Empire, and to experiment with plants from other parts of the world which had been disseminated by Kew. The site was small and was immediately threatened by the already palpable expansion of the city. Although nothing remains of this garden today, its location is recorded in the names of three streets: Kew Road, Kew Passage and Kew Points Road. In 1813 a second garden was established, this time on the banks of the Kalu Ganga at Kalutara, 'for the reception of economic plants'. In 1821 the decision was made to establish a much bigger botanic garden at Peradeniya on a peninsula lying at 450 metres above sea level in a horse-shoe bend of the Mahaweli, about 8 kilometres to the south-west of the city.

Like Kew, Peradeniya had begun its life as a royal pleasure garden, having first been used for that purpose at the end of the fourteenth century during the reign of Wickramabahu. During the eighteenth century it had served as the country seat of the last kings of Kandy. The British cleared the site of all surviving royal and religious buildings, and the already substantial plant collections at Kalutara were transferred over the following decade. The early plantings included cinnamon and coffee; the first tea bushes from China were established there in 1824. Today the Peradeniya Botanic Gardens cover an area of about 60 hectares and host a bewildering collection of indigenous and imported trees and shrubs. These include a magnificent Java Fig which spreads its huge branches over the Great Lawn, an improbable line of Cook's Pines which run along the bank of the Mahaweli, and an impressive avenue of palm trees.

A second botanic garden was established in 1860 at Hakgala near Nuwara Eliya at a height of 1,700 metres. Here the first aim was to grow chinchona, the source of the drug quinine, which was used in combating malaria – but later on the gardens were used to conduct experiments with temperate-zone plants and served as a plant nursery for the bungalow gardens of British tea planters.

In 1876 a third botanic garden was established at Henerathgoda near Gampaha with the express aim to propagate rubber seeds. Rubber trees were endemic to the Amazonian rainforests, but as rubber was becoming an increasingly valuable product the British were determined to break the South American monopoly on its production. In a feat of industrial espionage, a British agent smuggled seventy thousand seeds to Kew, where about three thousand seedlings were successfully propagated. Of these, two thousand were then shipped to Ceylon and planted at Henerathgoda. These in turn furnished the seedlings that were used to establish rubber plantations throughout the low country, as well as across British Asia from South India to Malaya.

Early experiments with plantation crops during the 1820s led to large-scale planting of coffee in the Kandyan highlands during the 1830s. The proliferation of coffee estates was encouraged by the land ordinances of 1841 and 1842, which empowered the colonial administration to sell what had hitherto been regarded as 'crown' or 'common' land to mainly European coffee planters. Thus the new estates encroached on

1 Sri Lanka – The Larger Garden

Above: The gardens of the Castlereagh Estate bungalow

Opposite from top left: Typical estate bungalow from the 1920s: Kotiyagala Estate, Bogolontalawa; The enclosed verandah; Summerhill Estate bungalow; The garden at Tientsin Estate

the traditional buffer lands of the Kandyan villages, threatening traditional farming and provoking deep resentment on the part of the local population. The clearances also represented the beginning of a massive assault on the natural landscape of the highlands in which primeval montane forests were felled and burnt, and precious soils were eroded and lost forever. The massive expansion of the plantations during the second half of the nineteenth century could be said to have changed the island's ecology irreversibly.

Between 1838 and 1843, more than a hundred plantations were opened up in the area around Kandy, and by 1846 Ceylon boasted more than five hundred coffee plantations covering a total area of 20,000 hectares. Other plantation crops such as indigo and sugar failed to achieve the same success, while cinnamon, for long a highly prized export, declined in the face of competition from Indian cassia. After 1850 there was considerable investment in coconut, particularly in the area around Kurunagala. Coffee meanwhile continued to thrive, and by 1875 there were more than 100,000 hectares under cultivation.

The rapid increase in plantation activity placed new demands on the island's transport infrastructure. An extensive road-building programme was launched after 1855, and the beginnings of a rail network were established during the 1860s. All this in turn led to an increased demand for labour, exacerbated by the fact that Sinhalese farmers were reluctant to give up their traditional way of life to work as plantation labourers. From the 1850s onwards,

increasing numbers of labourers were brought down to Ceylon from southern India. Although these were initially temporary and often seasonal visitors, as the century drew on there was an increasing tendency for them to settle permanently on the estates as indentured labourers.

The coffee bubble burst at the end of the 1870s with the onset of a leaf blight which spread quickly from plantation to plantation. However, the rapid and total eclipse of coffee led almost immediately to the emergence of three other main plantation crops: tea, which replaced coffee at higher altitudes; rubber, which was planted on a large scale after 1880; and coconut. Tea was labour-intensive, required relatively high capital investment and thus remained very much the preserve of larger foreign agencies, while rubber and coconut could be planted on a smaller scale and were developed by local investors, mainly low-country Sinhalese.

By the end of the nineteenth century, there were more than twelve hundred major tea estates, covering a quarter of a million hectares, most of them owned by foreign agencies and managed by an army of more than two thousand European planters. Other plantation sectors had grown apace: rubber estates, concentrated mainly in the south-western lowlands, covered an area similar to the tea estates, while coconut estates flourished in the triangle formed by Chilaw, Colombo and Matale, covering more than 400,000 hectares. At the time of independence in 1948, the area given over to plantation cultivation was estimated to have reached almost a million hectares or 15 per cent of Sri Lanka's total land area.

Above: A typical Kandyan manor house: Amunugama Walaawe, now the Kandy House Hotel

Opposite from top: A typical low-country coconut estate bungalow; A rubber tapper at work

The early coffee and tea planters were a tough breed of men, people who had gambled everything on the chance of wresting a livelihood, perchance a fortune, from the untested landscape of a faraway place. Many of them hailed from Scotland, a fact that is recorded in the names of numerous tea estates: Napier, Kinross, Elgin, Stratheden, Caledonia, Macduff, Clarendon, Stirling, Holyrood, Strathspey, Lammermoor, Strathellie and others. This first generation lived simple lives – they built crude bungalows of stone with thatched roofs, followed a solitary existence and took local women as their wives or concubines. (The Bawa brothers' own maternal grandmother was born Marion Campbell and was the daughter of a Scottish planter and his Sinhalese wife.)

Towards the end of the nineteenth century, however, as tea prospered, a new generation of planters emerged. Better educated, they brought wives with them from Britain. A new world sprang into being, one that echoed the life of provincial Scotland. There were racecourses, rugby fields, small nine-hole golf courses, simple Anglican chapels, and clubs where planters could meet to drink whisky and play cards while their wives chatted and planned the next tennis tournament or fancy-dress ball.

Each estate was centred on its factory and workshops, with the line houses of the workers usually clustered lower down the valley close to running water. The superintendent occupied the main bungalow, usually sited well away from the factory on a high knoll with views out across surrounding hills, while his assistants occupied lesser bungalows on equally favourable sites in other divisions of the estate. The bungalows were now built as elaborate pastiches of houses in the Home Counties or Scottish Lowlands. Walls were of cut stone or rubble finished with pebble-dash and punctuated by small-paned bay windows, while the shallow roofs were clad in timber shingle and crowned by clusters of brick chimneys. The main living rooms opened onto deep verandahs which were supported on timber columns and looked out towards the view.

Furniture was made up of robust items of local manufacture interspersed with more ornate pieces brought out from Victorian England. Tables were laid with cut glass, bone china and silver cutlery, and walls were hung with paintings of Highland cattle foraging in misty glens. Planters who, two decades earlier, would have sat at a rough table in their working breeches and scoffed a simple meal of rice and curry now dined in full evening dress by candlelight, waited on by white-gloved retainers who served up such culinary delights as 'mock turtle soup', 'steak and oyster pie' and 'crème caramel', all washed down with a fine claret.

The pride of every estate bungalow was its garden, often the creation of the superintendent's wife. A typical garden might extend over several hectares and be divided into a number of compartments. The main verandahs of the house opened on to neat lawns surrounded by flower beds and clumps of shrubs and trees. Steps and trellised arches led down to a lower terrace with a tennis court and croquet lawn, while at one side was the kitchen garden with rows of European vegetables and on the other the orchard, where apples and pears grew alongside mangoes and avocados. Below the formal gardens a network of footpaths meandered down through wooded glades to a stream with cascades and bathing pools.

Life on the lowland rubber and coconut estates echoed that in the hill country, though the estates were generally smaller and the managers more likely to be Ceylonese. As the plantation industry prospered, so the Ceylonese owners and managers built ever larger and more elaborate bungalows, sometimes echoing the traditional Sinhalese walaawe, or manor house, more often imitating or parodying the styles which had been adopted by the European planters in the hills. Many such houses are recorded in great detail in Arnold Wright's 1907 compendium *Twentieth Century Impressions of Ceylon*, a book which clearly illustrates how an emerging class of Ceylonese entrepreneurs lived in strange suspension between West and East. The lowland planters also cultivated elaborate gardens, though these were more likely to be stocked with indigenous plants and trees.

The strange world of the expatriate tea planters lasted barely a century. After independence, the older planters retired and returned to Britain to be replaced by a new generation of Sri Lankan planters. After 1970 the foreign-owned tea estates were all nationalized. Since then the shingle roofs of the bungalows have given way to corrugated-iron sheeting, and their croquet lawns have been turned into vegetable plots.

A NATION OF GARDENERS

The Sinhalese remain planters and gardeners at heart, and the Govigama, or farmer caste, is the biggest and most senior of their castes. Visitors to Sri Lanka will be struck by the geometrically ordered fields of emerald-green rice paddy, by the swaying groves of coconut palms and serried ranks of silver-trunked rubber trees, and by the clipped, carpeted hillsides of tea bushes. They will also be impressed by a visit to any of the three botanic gardens or to one of the private gardens that have recently been created, such as Sam Popham's Arboretum at Dambulla or Laki Senanayake's boulder fantasy at Diyabubula.

Private gardens in Colombo have shrunk in size during the past two decades, and many have retreated behind high walls, but their owners remain passionate gardeners and create miniature tropical landscapes on pocket-handkerchief plots. In the suburbs of the capital and in the provincial towns, a peep over a hedge or through a gate will often reveal exotic gardens of great beauty. Around Negombo, in particular, where there are large numbers of Catholics who have worked in Italy, an area that has come to be known as 'Little Sicily' is populated by modern, multi-gabled villas set in highly decorative gardens. In the outlying villages, a typical house is still set within its compound of carefully swept earth, shaded by trees and shrubs, and surrounded by a larger 'home garden' of fruit-bearing trees and bushes.

Hotels in Sri Lanka are also distinguished by the quality of their landscaping. One early hotel landscape which survives intact is that of the Sigiriya Village Hotel, which was laid out by Bevis Bawa in the early 1980s and planned as a series of village clusters, each focused on a stylized evocation of a traditional landscape. Another, dating from the same period, is the Habarana Lodge by Ismeth Raheem, which is set beside a large reservoir in a grove of specially planted trees. Geoffrey Bawa's Kandalama Hotel (1992) was inspired by the nearby citadel of Sigiriya and was built along the face of a cliff, surrounded by jungle and overlooking an ancient reservoir.

Recent hotel design seeks to confront visitors with the varied natural landscapes of Sri Lanka, and a number of travel firms are now concentrating on ecologically friendly tourism. The Tea Factory Hotel near Nuwara Eliya has been converted from an old tea factory and is set within a working tea estate, while the Dilmah Tea Company operates a chain of estate bungalows in which visitors can experience the planters' life at first hand. Lalyn Collure's Boulder Garden Hotel has been inserted into a cluster of caves and massive boulders on the edge of the ancient Sinharajah Forest, and offers its guests an astonishing opportunity to commune with tropical nature. Ruckman Fonseka's Galapita Hotel, near Buttola in the south-east of the island, is set directly on the rocky banks of the Menik Ganga and recreates the ambience of a typical dry-zone village.

The people of Sri Lanka are rediscovering the pleasures of landscape and are reviving a culture of garden-making that was suppressed during four centuries of foreign rule. After the destructive exploitation of the countryside which accompanied the colonial and post-colonial development of the island, they are waking up to the need to conserve their precious landscape for the benefit of future generations.

II
Two Brothers

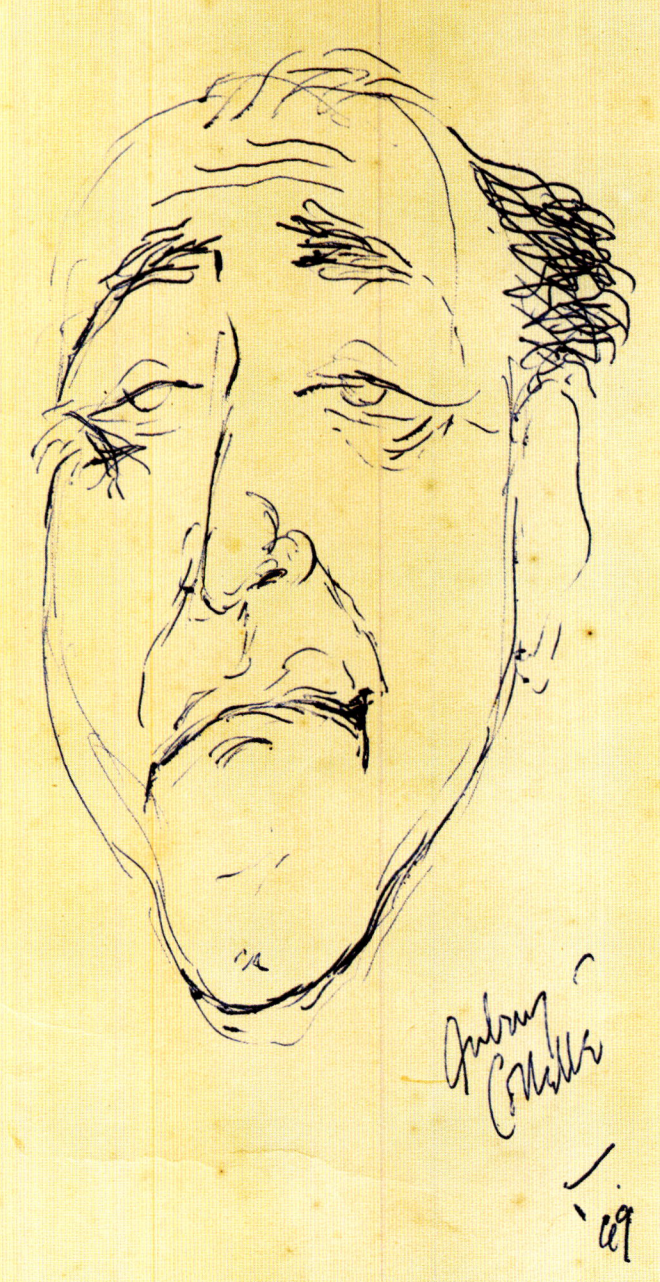

'I left home at the age of seventeen when Geoffrey was only seven and Geoffrey left for Cambridge when he was eighteen. So it was only natural that we were more or less strangers at the time of his return: I, eastern in outlook, and Geoffrey British.' BEVIS BAWA, 1990

BAWAS AND SCHRADERS

Bevis and Geoffrey Bawa were born in Colombo, the only sons of Benjamin and Bertha Bawa. Benjamin was a successful and wealthy lawyer whose ancestors had been Moors from Beruwela. His father, Ahamadu Bawa, who was a proctor in Galle, had travelled to England to complete his legal studies in London and there had met and married a lady of French Huguenot descent called Georgina Ablett. Benjamin, the oldest of their six children, had been born in 1865 and educated at Royal College, Colombo's most prestigious boys' school. He then was articled to James van Langenberg, a leading lawyer of the time, and later was called to the Colombo Bar.

Benjamin Bawa was one of the most successful Colombo lawyers of his day. Handsome, charismatic and a keen sportsman, he could pass easily through the different compartments of the town's highly stratified society. In 1893 he obtained a commission in the Ceylon Light Infantry, a part-time militia that boasted a mixture of European and Ceylonese officers.

In 1906 Benjamin bought Chapman House, one of two linked villas which occupied a large garden at the south end of Darley Road opposite Hyde Park. At the time, Darley Road (now a busy thoroughfare lined with offices and factories) was a quiet, tree-lined avenue running parallel to the eastern end of Beira Lake and was conveniently situated between the new suburb of Cinnamon Gardens and the legal district of Hultsdorf.

Two years later, Benjamin married Bertha Schrader, the daughter of a wealthy Burgher called Frederick Justus Schrader. The Schraders claimed descent from a German mercenary called Julius Schrader who had arrived in Ceylon at the beginning of the eighteenth century. Frederick Justus had been born in Colombo in 1829 and become a successful planter. He owned large coconut estates at Wester Seaton and Kimbulapitiya near Negombo, as well as a cinnamon plantation that stretched from what is now Lipton Circus to Borella Junction in Colombo. After the death of his first wife, Frederick married Elizabeth Harriet Campbell. Together they had five children, the eldest of

Opposite: From the Brief Visitors' Book: Bevis and Geoffrey Bawa drawn by Aubrey Collette (a founder member of the 43 Group)

Far left: Chapman House in Darley Road, the Bawas' Colombo home, *c.* 1920.
Left: Wester Seaton, the Schrader family's estate bungalow near Negombo

Right: Mr and Mrs Bawa in the family dog cart, Chapman House, c. 1907. Below: Bertha and Benjamin Bawa with baby Bevis, 1909

Opposite from top: Benjamin Bawa in lawyer's rig; Bevis and Geoffrey with the family Daimler, c. 1928

whom, Bertha Marion Campbell Schrader, was born in 1876.

When Frederick Justus died, he left his various Negombo estates to the five children from his second marriage. Bertha and her three sisters, all of whom eventually married lawyers, sold their shares to their brother Fred, who continued to run the estates and lived in the bungalow at Kimbulapitiya.

Benjamin and Bertha Bawa, though no longer in the first flush of youth when they married, cut dashing figures in Colombo society. Bertha used some of her inheritance to buy the adjoining half of Chapman House, with the result that the combined gardens covered nearly a hectare.

BEVIS'S CHILDHOOD

The Bawas' first son, Bevis, was born a bouncing 7 kilos, according to his own, not always reliable, memoirs. When he was shown to his mother, she reportedly swooned and cried, 'Take it away!' while his father said, 'A fine neck for high collars!' Bevis grew up surrounded by ayas and servants – at the time of his birth there was a total of seventeen staff working in Chapman House – while his parents followed their busy daily rounds. His mother spent her days calling on friends or meeting up with her three married sisters; his father combined running a busy practice with his duties in the Ceylon Light Infantry, and in 1918 became aide-de-camp to Sir William Manning, the new British governor. Benjamin would ride before breakfast, work in his chambers during the morning, take an early lunch, attend court during the afternoon and spend the early evening at one or other of his clubs. At night both parents were swept up in a whirl of social engagements. Bevis added further details in his unpublished memoirs:

Wednesday, however, was my father's 'at home' day, when I, 'his wonderful son and heir' had to make a display of my prowess as a horseman, mounting and dismounting and riding a skinny docile pony, while my nice uncles, being civilised gentlemen cheered and clapped loudly and said: 'What a splendid young fella!'

In 1915 the Bawas acquired their first motor car, a Sunbeam Tourer, and employed a Malay chauffeur called Rahim. At that time the roads were narrow and badly surfaced, and filled with ponderous bullock carts and straying cattle. It was thought best to travel in the early morning before sunrise. In his memoirs Bevis recalled the family's first journey to visit his Uncle Fred in Negombo, a distance of 30 kilometres:

There was a great activity at home preparing for the journey. The whole staff assembled at 4.30 in the morning and the packing took at least half an hour: thermos flasks, a tiffin basket, two spare wheels, an extra tyre and a tube, canisters of petrol and all sorts of odds and ends. The bags had to be strapped to the luggage carrier at the back and covered with canvas on account of the dust. The carbide headlights and the side oil lights were lit and the engine was cranked by the washing dobhi. My mother's maid had brought along some sliced potatoes to rub on the windscreen in the event of rain, wipers being non-existent at the time. Once the engine was turning Rahim sounded the bulb horn and we all entered the car. My mother adjusted her dust-veil and with a waving of hands and the shedding of not a few tears by female members of the staff, the engine struck up a beautiful hum and we moved off. For the most part we sailed along at a steady 25 kph with occasional spurts of up to 40 kph. After an hour the sun came up over the rice fields and we stopped to eat hot egg hoppers from a wayside kade. Finally, after almost three hours we arrived at Uncle Fred's estate at Kimbulapitiya and were greeted by my uncle, his wife, their son Ronnie and as large a staff as had seen us off.

The Kimbulapitiya bungalow sat on a low hill surrounded by coconut and cinnamon. A typical low-country estate bungalow of the mid-nineteenth century, it had a courtyard plan similar to that of a Kandyan manor house but executed in the 'Anglo-Dutch' style. Visitors arrived at a generous *porte-cochère* supported by white Tuscan columns and a deep verandah which opened to the main sitting and dining room. The bedrooms and their dependencies occupied two parallel wings which ran along either side of the main hall and continued to enclose the main courtyard at the rear.

LOSING A FATHER AND GAINING A BROTHER

Everything changed for Bevis after his tenth year, when his mother gave birth to a second son who was christened Geoffrey Manning Bawa in honour of his godfather, Governor Manning. Bevis now found himself playing second fiddle to a blond, blue-eyed baby. A couple of years later, his father fell ill and was diagnosed with Bright's disease, a chronic ailment of the kidneys. In 1922 the whole family travelled to Britain in the vain hope of finding a cure. After spending several months in London, they moved to a nursing home near Harrogate, where Benjamin died the following spring. Bevis had lost the dashing soldier-father whom he so idolized and gained a rival sibling.

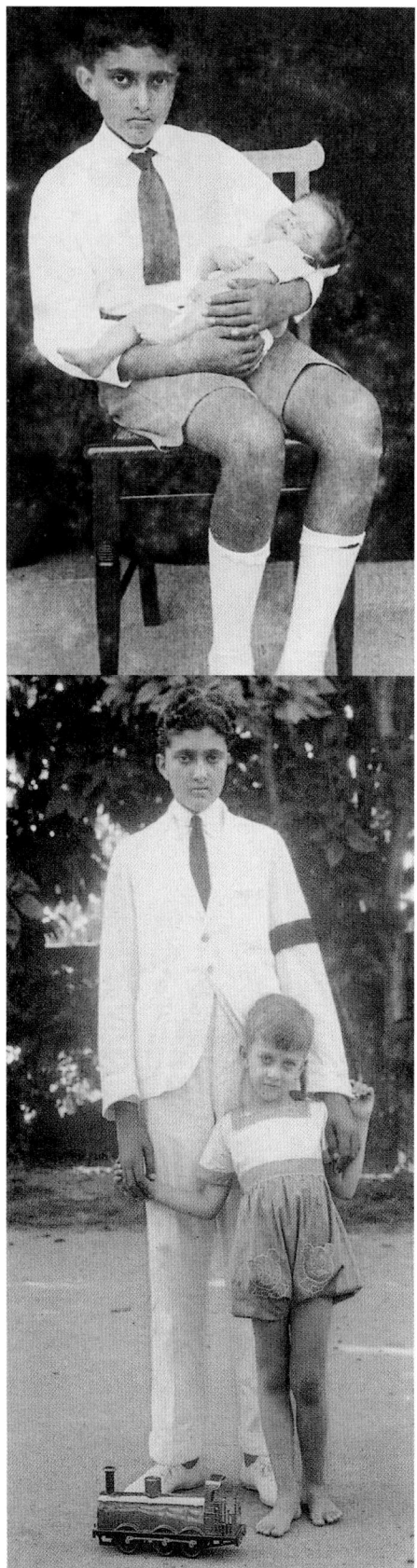

After their return to Ceylon, Bertha withdrew from society and divided her time between Chapman House, which she shared with Benjamin's two spinster sisters, Violet and Rose, and her brother's estate at Kimbulapitiya. Still a wealthy woman, she continued to live in some style. In 1928 she imported a yellow sleeve-valved Daimler and passed the Sunbeam on to Bevis. Two years later she gifted him with a new six-cylinder Humber for his twenty-first birthday. Bertha enjoyed travelling and made regular motor tours of Ceylon, as well as several trips to Europe.

BEVIS'S SCHOOLDAYS

As a child Bevis had been taught by a series of private tutors, but in 1922 he enrolled at Royal College, where (as he put it in his memoirs) '... they tried to teach me a lot of gibberish such as Latin, Geometry and Algebra, which I knew would be utterly useless to me.' His lack of interest in studying soon became apparent, and he spent most of his lessons making caricatures of his teachers. He was shy and very conscious of his height – he was more than 1.8 metres (6 feet) tall at the age of thirteen – and made few school friends. Indeed the closest friend of his childhood was Arthur van Langenberg, the grandson of his father's mentor and a pupil at the rival St Joseph's College. The two boys had played together as children, and both had lost their fathers. Arthur, however, was a precocious youth, widely read and very knowledgeable about art. He would later become an important stage designer and as a teenager was already organizing variety shows in his home with Bevis roped in as stage manager.

Bevis's most vivid memory of his schooldays was the visit of the Prince of Wales in 1922. All his classmates, loyal subjects of the Empire, were lined up to cheer and wave small Union Jacks as the Prince drove past their school. Later, when Benjamin Bawa entertained the royal visitor at Chapman House for tea and tennis, Bevis was disappointed to discover that he was a mediocre tennis player but was most impressed by the fact that he threw away his cigarettes after only a few puffs. When the guests had left, Bevis collected all the butts and smoked them in the lavatory.

A PLANTER AND SOLDIER

By the time he was seventeen, Bevis had fallen so far behind with his studies that he was relegated to a class called 'The Remove'. The school motto was 'Learn or Depart', and he decided to follow the latter option. His mother, despairing at his lack of scholastic ambition, decided that, as there was little hope of him becoming a lawyer, he should follow another family tradition and become a planter. So she persuaded him to take over the running of a rubber estate near Aluthgama which she had inherited from her husband and christened 'Brief'. After spending a year learning the ropes, Bevis installed himself there at the end of 1928.

In the same year, following in his father's footsteps, he joined the Ceylon Light Infantry. The CLI was a local volunteer reserve which was never taken seriously either by the British or by the people who served in it. Getting a commission in those days was a fairly simple matter: the commanding officer selected candidates on the basis of gentlemanly bearing and their ability to settle their bar bills; family connections played a big role, whereas educational qualifications or physical fitness were of little consequence. The regiment had a total of thirty officers, all part-time and drawn mainly from the business and planting community. Half of them were British, all of them were in it for the 'fun and glory'. Bevis's extensive recollections of life in the CLI dwelt almost entirely on annual camps, botched war games, ritual raggings, dinner parties and drunken brawls.

As well as being almost 2 metres in height, Bevis was now of manly bearing. In 1934 he was appointed aide-de-camp to the governor, a position which brought great kudos and a small stipend, and which he retained for eighteen years, serving four successive incumbents: Sir Edward Stubbs, Sir Andrew Caldecott, Sir Henry Monck-Mason-Moore and Viscount Soulbury. At the independence celebrations in 1948 Bevis had to accompany Monck-Mason-Moore on the processional drive past in an open-topped car. The governor was a small man who almost disappeared from view behind the upholstery, whereas Bevis in his plumed hat towered above him and waved graciously to the passing crowds on his behalf.

A VOYAGE TO CHINA

In 1934 Bevis contracted tuberculosis and, after a course of treatment at Colombo General Hospital, was recommended to take a sea voyage. His mother decided that she and Geoffrey would accompany him, and booked a three-month round trip to the Far East with the Blue Funnel Line. Although Bevis described the voyage in his memoirs and Geoffrey also reminisced about it, neither made any mention of the other. They sailed on the SS *Aeneas* and visited Penang, Singapore, China and Japan. Bevis's memories were mainly of people: Captain Hatfield with his 'nautical, weather-beaten, spider-webbed face'; Brigadier Brickman, a fellow passenger who wore 'a monocle in his right eye while his wife wore one in her left and their daughter who always walked between them, wore spectacles'; the handsome pageboys in Shanghai's Cathay Hotel with their glamorous uniforms and pill-box caps set at an angle.

Bertha Bawa could trade on her husband's connections, which meant, for instance, that the three were given an official reception by the governor in Hong Kong. But their equivocal position as Eurasians was often made apparent. Thus when Bevis offered to buy the brigadier a drink on board the *Aeneas*, the old soldier emitted

a muffled explosion of distaste, rapidly crashed into reverse gear and vanished. Later the captain told me that old Brickman had barged into his cabin to complain about the discipline on his ship and the fact that one of the Indian deck-hands had had the brass to offer him a drink at the bar.

Geoffrey, only fifteen at the time, had very different memories. In 1997, in conversation with Channa Daswatte, he said:

I remember going to China. I remember vaguely, walking through dusty Chinese squares, yellow walls, big doors. I don't think at the time that one assessed

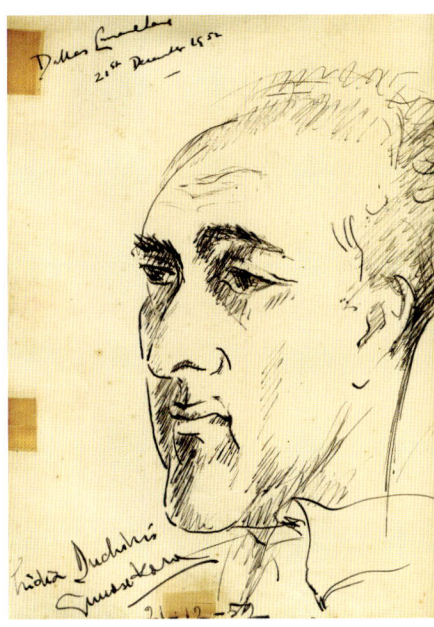

Opposite from top: Bevis Bawa with baby Geoffrey, 1919; Bevis and Geoffrey Bawa after the death of their father, c. 1923

Above from top: Bevis Bawa in his CLI officer's uniform; Bevis Bawa drawn by Lidia Duchini (Italian sculptor, client and friend of Geoffrey Bawa). Left: Geoffrey and Bevis with the Sunbeam, c. 1930

11 Two Brothers 37

Above from top: Geoffrey with his Meccano, *c.* 1932; In front of a ha-ha – Geoffrey Bawa in England, 1938; Geoffrey Bawa in Italy, 1956

these as such ... but it all gave me a feeling of pleasure, because one enjoyed the whole journey. I remember the Summer Palace and that great marble boat, pretending to be afloat ... and lots of long corridors, galleries of red lacquer.

GEOFFREY IN EUROPE

Geoffrey, ten years younger than Bevis, grew up in Chapman House, administered to by his mother, two aunts and a galaxy of servants, including his aya Ensa, who remained with him until her death in the 1980s, and a personal valet called Miguel. Geoffrey was a serious boy who spent long hours making machines out of Meccano and playing with his extensive Hornby Dublo railway network.

Geoffrey was no happier at Royal College than his brother had been, but he was more studious, and in 1937 he enrolled as a student at the University of Colombo. His mother expected him to follow in his father's footsteps and become a lawyer. At the end of 1938 she sent him to England, where he applied to the University of Cambridge and was offered a place to read English at St Catherine's College for the following October.

Early in 1939, Geoffrey went to Paris to stay with a distant cousin called Georgette Camille, the granddaughter of a sister of his paternal grandmother, Georgina Ablett. Georgette was a successful writer who had specialized in translating English novelists such as Virginia Woolf, and was a well-known figure in Parisian literary circles. Through her Geoffrey met some of the most famous artists and writers of the day. After springtime in Paris, he travelled south and, oblivious to the threat of war, spent the summer of 1939 in Italy before returning to London on the eve of the war.

Geoffrey had felt an outsider in Colombo, but Cambridge seemed to welcome his eccentricities. It drew him out of his shell, and he developed a wide circle of friends, gaining a reputation for entertaining conversation and cutting wit.

Handsome and exceptionally tall, he cut a dashing figure, striding round the town in a long black cloak with a gold topped-cane. His rooms in King's Parade were much admired, and he developed a reputation as a man of taste. Most people took him for a European, and he did little to disabuse them, often referring to mythical French grandmothers and Russian aunts, and claiming to be the illegitimate son of an 'aristocratic British planter'.

Several of his friends belonged to the minor aristocracy, and he was often invited to their country houses for weekends. One particular friend, Guy Strutt, was the son of Lord Rayleigh, whose family owned Terling Place in Essex and Beaufront Castle in Northumberland. As Geoffrey observed, 'It was during my time in Cambridge that I grew to love the English country house and its landscaped park.'

In 1942, having successfully completed his degree, Geoffrey moved to London to study for the Bar, sharing a flat in Belgravia with Guy Strutt. It was at this time that he bought his first Rolls Royce, a Phantom One Tourer. Soon after the end of the war in 1945, he and Strutt drove down to Italy and stayed with Guy's aunt in a villa at Cola di Lazise overlooking Lake Garda. An architect friend of the aunt took the young Sri Lankan under his wing and organized excursions, introducing him to the architecture of Andrea Palladio and to the gardens of Lombardy and the Veneto. The visit awakened in Geoffrey his first conscious interest in architecture and garden-making, as well as a love for Italy.

THE DEATH OF BERTHA BAWA

By 1945 the effects of the war and Geoffrey's long absence were taking their toll on the Bawa family fortunes, and Bertha was in poor health. Bevis sent urgent messages to Geoffrey throughout that year, alerting him to his mother's decline and warning him that he could no longer expect her to support his expensive lifestyle, though these seem to have gone unheeded. Late in 1945 Bertha suffered a stroke and was moved to Wycherly Nursing Home in Buller's Road. Finally, in January 1946, Bevis persuaded his brother to come home and, using his influence with the governor, secured him a seat on a military transport plane which flew him via Malta, Cairo and Bombay.

Geoffrey moved back into Chapman House and joined the law firm of Noel Gratiaen, a former friend and colleague of his father. His Rolls Royce had been shipped from England, and it gave him great pleasure to drive it down Darley Road to the courts in full lawyer's rig. But he was bored by the law and feared that his incompetence would result in the wrongful punishment of an innocent man.

When Bertha Bawa died in April 1946, she left her property to be divided between her two sons. But the effects of war, her long illness and Geoffrey's profligacy had indeed taken their toll, and the estate was straddled with debts and death duties. This was the first time that Bevis and Geoffrey had spent any time together as adults, and they found that they had little in common. As Bevis recalled in his memoirs,

I left home at the age of seventeen when Geoffrey was only seven and Geoffrey left for Cambridge when he was eighteen. So it was only natural that we were more or less strangers at the time of his return: I, eastern in outlook, and Geoffrey British. Geoffrey was happier with Europeans, hardly remembering his few school friends in Ceylon. His whole life was tied up with the arts, beauty and culture: good taste in everything from vintage cars to snuff boxes. He avoided anything that could be depressing, such as sickness and sorrow, misery and squalor. When he had to deal with unpleasant things he faced them with the stiff upper lip typical of the stoic Britisher of old.

In March 1989, when he was dictating his memoirs, Bevis wrote to the architect C. Anjalendran about his brother:

I have started my memoirs and I have to bring my brother in to them at some stage. As you are a great admirer I feel that you are the best person (to help). Though Geoffrey and I are dearly fond of each other we are strangers and therefore, to avoid upsetting each other, communicate through third parties. I don't know much about Geoffrey's brilliant career, but I remember seeing a book in which Geoffrey was described as one of the best architects in the world. Let me know all such details. Don't tell Geoffrey about my request. He knows, I don't know how, that I am writing my life story. In writing about him I intend to leave out all his weaknesses, only telling about his extraordinary charisma, which enables him to get all he wants and desires.

Above from top: Portrait of Bertha Bawa, c. 1940; An ageing Bevis Bawa, c. 1982; An ageing Geoffrey Bawa at Lunuganga, c. 1995. Left: Two Rolls Royces for two brothers, Brief, 1948

III

Brief

'... and Brief is Paradise: it is Shangri-la, a glimpse of Nirvana – call it what you will after you have been to see it ...'   ROBIN MAUGHAM, C.1974

As with so many episodes in Bawa family history, the purchase of the rubber estate near Aluthgama is shrouded in myth. Bevis himself recorded three different versions of how he came to own the place and how it got its name. It seems, however, that Benjamin Bawa assembled the estate over a period of years using money from unpaid legal briefs and that Bertha inherited it after her husband's death. The estate was originally called Dikbedde, but she renamed it to mark its provenance. Covering 80 hectares, it occupied an area of high ground which rose out of the flood plain of the Bentota River.

Having never been an autonomous estate, Brief lacked a factory or a sizeable bungalow. Mrs Bawa installed a temporary manager, an Irishman called Lang, with instructions that he extend the existing bungalow. While it was being renovated, Bevis spent six months of 1927 learning about the management of coconut estates from his Uncle Fred at Kimbulapitiya and then, in the following year, working as a 'creeper' or apprentice at Eladuwa. Eladuwa had been managed at the turn of the century by Alfred Bawa, a younger brother of Benjamin, who named one of its divisions 'Ablett' in honour of their mother. The current manager was Vicky van Langenberg, a distant relative of Bevis's friend Arthur, and Bevis lived with him and his wife Eila in the estate's main bungalow. Vicky taught Bevis the basics of how to run a large estate while Eila introduced him to the social etiquette of estate life. During his six-month apprenticeship he was expected to call, one by one, on all the planters in the Kalutara District, of whom there were about seventy-five, most of them British. In this way Bevis came to see a broad cross-section of planters' bungalows and gardens.

Bevis was now deemed ready to take over his estate and his mother presented him with the keys to the family Sunbeam, his father's golf clubs and – servants being considered as little more than chattels – his father's valet. As he put it in his memoirs,

At this age I had a rather exaggerated idea of myself and now look back with amusement at my foolish vanities. I used to walk around my estate of eighty hectares as if it were eight hundred. I wore a double-terrel hat, a cream silk shirt with the collar turned up, corduroy jodhpurs (though there wasn't a horse in the whole district) and polished top boots. Ahead walked the kangany (overseer) wearing gold earrings, behind me ran a small lad with a coconut shell containing liquid salt to keep the impertinent leeches away from the mahamahitiya (master).

I felt I was building a little kingdom of my own and was a law unto myself. I had forty human beings under me, half of them Indian Tamils. The others were Sinhalese villagers who either didn't work or didn't to turn up to work, which was very sensible because each of them had his own little bit of land. I saw to it that both communities mixed and were on excellent terms with each-other.

THE DEVELOPMENT OF THE GARDEN

The long and detailed memoir Bevis dictated to his friend Mervyn Nanayakara in 1989 is filled mainly with anecdotes about people and tells little

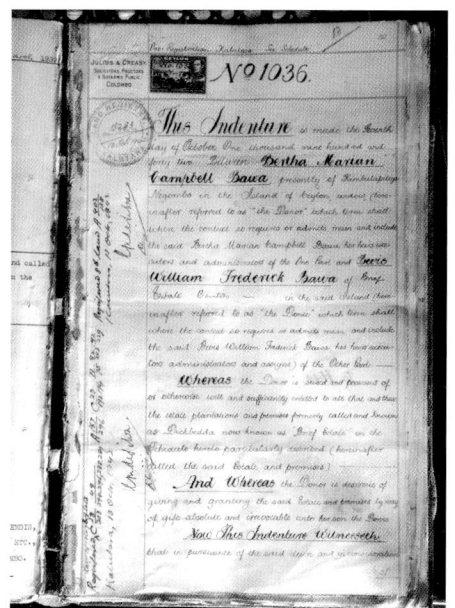

Opposite: Figure of a boy in the Spanish Court, by Bevis Bawa

Above from top: The deed of transfer of Brief from Bertha Bawa to Bevis Bawa, 1942; Cartoon from *Briefly by Bevis* (1985) showing Bevis arriving as a 'creeper' at the Eladuwa Estate in 1928

Above: The Schrader family's Kimbulapitiya Estate bungalow. Below from left: Bevis Bawa's caricature of the four governors under whom he served: Sir Edward Stubbs, Sir Andrew Caldecott, Sir Henry Monck-Mason-Moore and Viscount Soulbury. Bevis Bawa and Hilden Sansoni are behind Soulbury; Aides-de-camp with the governor general: Bevis Bawa (third from right) and Hilden Sansoni (second from right) behind Viscount Soulbury

Opposite from top: Georgette Camille and Victor Chapin at Brief in 1949; Early views of Brief

about the development of his garden. For a time he made a serious attempt to manage the rubber estate, though it soon became clear that he lacked the self-discipline which the monotonous regime demanded. Growing bored with the routine and isolation of estate life, as the 1930s progressed he devoted himself more and more to the Ceylon Light Infantry and to his duties as aide-de-camp to the British governor. These required him to spend more time in Colombo, where he was happy to enjoy a cushioned life in his mother's house in Darley Road. The day-to-day running of Brief was delegated to a superintendent, and it soon started to lose money.

After war broke out, Bevis was called up for active service, and, following a short spell in the Hill Country, was stationed in Trincomalee as part of a force set up to defend eastern Ceylon against Japanese invasion. In 1941 the house in Darley Road was requisitioned by the government, and Bertha went to live at Brief, where she remained until her death in 1946. At first she lived in the main bungalow, but Bevis built her a two-room annex on the north side of the house so that she would not be disturbed by his visitors. In 1942 he resigned his commission, supposedly because of ill health, and was placed on reserve. He returned to Brief and lived there with his mother; in that year she transferred the ownership of the estate into his name. It was during this period, perhaps with her encouragement, that he started to take a more active interest in the garden.

Bevis's first moves in planning the garden were determined by what was there already – the position of the bungalow and the fall of the land – and his immediate sources of inspiration were the countless estate gardens which he had visited as a 'creeper'. The garden at this time was still confined to the immediate area around the bungalow and was entirely hemmed in by rubber trees. A driveway skirted the north side of the property, and cars could come as far as the main west-facing verandah. Bevis's first radical act was to clear away about two hundred rubber trees and open views from the west of the house. He had calculated that he was producing rubber at 9 cents per pound and selling it for 6, and convinced himself that he would actually save money if he replaced rubber with garden. In his memoirs in 1989, he wrote:

I told my mother that if we cut down two hundred trees we would lose less. Her mathematical capability was as shocking as my own and she said 'You seem to have a point there, but let's not go into it too deeply. However, I agree that a view from your house is absolutely essential!'

Bevis's childhood playmate Arthur van Langenberg was now making a name for himself in the theatre. They both had close friends in the 43 Group, a constellation of artists which orbited around the photographer Lionel Wendt, and hovered at its fringe, keeping in close touch with new ideas in the arts. Arthur was interested in garden design and was a regular visitor to Brief, where he helped with the planning of the garden, encouraging Bevis to adopt a theatrical or scenographic approach and suggesting that the place be conceived as a series of discrete spaces or tableaux, each with its own mood and character, to be moved through in a sequence. Bevis diverted the driveway and created a circus to the south-east of the house for visitors' cars. From there a small gate connected with the lower part of the garden while a door opened onto a small staircase which led directly into the house. The area to the west of the bungalow was now developed as a composition of three spatial sequences which radiated down from the north lawn and were then reconnected by meandering pathways on the lower slopes of the hill.

It was becoming clear to Bevis that his mother's fortune was beginning to run out and that Brief was too small an establishment from which to generate a substantial livelihood out of rubber. In 1944 he started a small dairy and chicken farm on a corner of the estate. At this time he also established a plant nursery, initially to propagate plants for his own expanding garden, later to sell to the new garden-owning middle classes of Colombo. Over the next four years all the important elements of the Brief garden were put in place, so that when his brother Geoffrey came to stay in 1948 the broad picture of what we see today had been established.

By 1950, the dairy farm had foundered, but the plant nursery and landscape business were a great success. As the 1950s progressed the gardens became famous, and large numbers of visitors flocked from the new suburbs of Colombo to see them and to buy (or sometimes steal) plants. Bevis was hailed as a talented garden planner and, together with Arthur, started to operate a landscape-design consultancy. As their fame spread, they were regularly called upon to design gardens for foreign embassies, hotels, private houses and country estates. Among their completed gardens were those of the Bentota Rest House and the Bank of Ceylon in Jaffna (both undertaken in the 1950s). Later Bevis collaborated with a young friend called Cedric de Silva, who worked alongside two gardeners from Brief called Karunadasa and Ari Seneviratne to landscape the Sigiriya Village Hotel (1980), a design which still survives. Surprisingly, Bevis was never invited by his brother to work as a landscape consultant on any of his architectural projects, and it is said that Geoffrey went so far as to instruct clients never to employ him.

As the garden flourished, Bevis played host to a group of Sri Lankan artists who in their different fields were busy inventing new art forms for a newly independent Sri Lanka: the batik artist Ena de Silva, the designer Barbara Sansoni, the artist Laki Senanayake, the dancers Chitrasena and Vajira and, of course, Bevis's brother Geoffrey. Bevis operated as their impresario, as the hub of their circle, and Brief served as their meeting place.

From his schooldays, Bevis had always drawn caricatures of the people around him, though he was reluctant to show his drawings to others. Finally, in June 1981, Harry Pieris of the 43 Group persuaded him to stage an exhibition at the Sapumal Foundation in Colombo. For this occasion more than a hundred drawings were miraculously flushed out from various private collections, revealing the true extent of Bevis's talent.

After 1948 Bevis became a well-known figure in Colombo society and acquired a reputation as a wit and raconteur. Denzil Pieris, the editor of the *Sunday Observer*, asked him to commit some of his stories to print, and he began to contribute a weekly series of articles which lampooned the great and the good. These became very popular,

and in 1985, some twenty-five years after they first appeared, a selection was published in a book under the title *Briefly by Bevis*. The book opened with a typical stroke of Bevis humour:

'Oh wad some Power the giftie gie us
To see oursels as others see us!'
ROBERT BURNS

'But how much better if by spells
Others see us as we see ourselves!'
BEVIS BAWA

Bevis regaled his readers with stories from his days as an officer in the CLI and as aide-de-camp in King's House. One typical piece was entitled 'The day we shot the "Japs" at Trinco':

And then came the Raid about which songs have been composed and we made such a hoo-ha, while Britain had them every day for breakfast, tea and dinner. The Japs had bombed Colombo and it was only to be expected that we would be next in line. The Colonel assembled all and sundry and gave an unforgettable 'pep talk' on what was expected of us.

I was alone in the middle of breakfast when sirens shrieked and I rushed off towards my slit trench nibbling my unfinished sausage. An excited young officer shouted 'Run, sir Run!' as he dashed past me at great speed. I have never run in my life, being top heavy and badly balanced, and I thought: 'Let the bloody little fool think that I'm just being brave!' When they did come they dropped their bombs from a great height and hit every damned thing they wanted with pin-point accuracy. I'm sure that if they had played fair and flown within range we would have shot them all out of the sky with our .303 rifles.

During the 1960s ill-health began to restrict Bevis's lifestyle. Like his mother he suffered from an acute form of diabetes, and this began to affect his mobility. Later he contracted glaucoma, and his eyesight started to deteriorate. Together these two afflictions made it increasingly difficult to run his landscape business, and his income plummeted. In 1969 he asked friends to recommend someone who could act as his personal assistant and secretary and was introduced to Dooland de Silva, an ex-schoolteacher from a neighbouring village. Dooland became his companion and later helped to revive the landscape business.

Slowly Bevis's world began to shrink until it was reduced to the confines of his garden. He had inherited a love of motor cars from his parents; a montage of photographs in the corridor at Brief shows the twenty vehicles that he had owned since his teens. These included the Humber and Sunbeam which his mother had given him, his mother's Daimler, the Rolls Royce Phantom he bought from his brother, and his favourite Mini-Moke with the 'red devil' insignia on the bonnet. By the end of the 1970s he could no longer afford the upkeep of a car, and his last one was sold in 1980. Thereafter Bevis very much lived the life of an invalid, administered to by Dooland and his loyal servants, becoming nearly blind and more or less bedridden during his final years.

Bevis remained generous to the last and gave even when there was nothing left to give. By the time of his death the estate had shrunk to 30 acres. In his will he settled the house and its 7 surrounding acres on Dooland and divided the remaining 22 acres between five of his closest helpers.

VISITORS TO BRIEF

During the eighty years of its existence, Brief has drawn thousands of visitors from around the world, some famous, some infamous. Wherever he went, Bevis Bawa attracted attention, in part because of his extreme height and physical presence, in part because of his charm and charisma. When he travelled he made new friends easily, and he always invited them to drop in and see him. Many did just that. For years he treated the Galle Face Hotel as his Colombo home and its terrace as his sitting room. There he would strike up conversations with anybody and everybody, including, over the years, Douglas Fairbanks and Mary Pickford, Caneira the boxer, Aldous Huxley, the Duke of Bedford, Gregory Peck, Alec Guinness and Laurence Olivier, and he invited them all to see his garden. Visitors included Vivien Leigh and Peter Finch, Ingrid Queen Mother of Denmark and Agatha Christie. As Bevis noted in his memoirs in 1989, most enthused, 'ninety out of hundred employing the word "paradise" while absent-mindedly crushing the mosquitoes on their arms and legs'. Some offered advice, like the lady who suggested to Bevis that he fill the cascading pools with fish. 'A gorgeous idea but sadly the cranes and kingfishers would eat them.' 'But you could cover them with chicken wire.' 'How ghastly!' 'And you must paint them a variety of colours, like a rainbow.' An American visitor suggested opening a casino, and an English lady wanted to stage open-air Shakespeare on the terraces. Others, like the man who said he'd been walking around for more than an hour and hadn't managed to find what there was to see, were clearly disappointed.

DONALD FRIEND

The painter Donald Friend lived at Brief from 1957 until 1962 and kept a detailed record of his life in the form of a beautifully illustrated, handwritten diary. He had first met Bevis in 1949 on board a ship called the *Toscana* which was en route from Sydney to Genoa via Colombo. As he described it in his diary for 1949:

Amongst the new passengers two are outstanding – a very French woman called Georgette travelling with her cousin, a Sinhalese, who is the tallest man I've ever seen. She is a very sophisticated Parisian type, and claims to be a friend of a host of people such as André Gide, Masson, Picasso, Pignon etc. He is almost indescribable – a languid too-English voice – amusing, drawling, lazy – a descendant of the kings of Kandy.

The tall Sinhalese was of course Bevis, while Georgette was Bevis's cousin Georgette Camille. Georgette's claims were all true, while Bevis, who always followed the maxim that a well-told lie is worth a thousand truths, was telling fibs: he wasn't Sinhalese, and he certainly wasn't descended from the kings of Kandy.

They next met in September 1953 when Donald was returning to Australia from a tour of Europe and his ship made a brief stop in Colombo. As Donald noted in his diary,

Bevis's car was at the wharf and we drove down to his estate at Brief. The house and gardens were like a dream. I can't imagine anything more lovely. The house was full of tall rooms, open to the garden, exquisitely furnished, an air of tropical aristocracy, of time and comfort. Everywhere the light splashing sound of fountains. Silent servants came bearing drinks. And he himself was as ever charming, diverting, original, the amusing host. I was consumed with admiration. 'You must come back', he said, 'Come and stay for as long as you like.' – There is nothing I'd like to do more.

During his time at Brief, Donald Friend produced some of his best work. Bevis was a charming, though sometimes irritating, host who gathered together an ever-changing group of friends, while Donald attracted a steady stream of visitors from Europe and Australia. Under their joint management the garden became both a beacon for travellers and a meeting place for artists and writers.

Bevis was by now running a lucrative plant nursery and a successful landscape design consultancy. He co-opted Donald to help him with a number of projects, including the refurbishment of the Bentota Rest House. Together they began to experiment with ways to make garden ornaments and statuary, beginning (as Donald noted in his diary in 1957) with a pair of new gateposts at the entrance to Brief:

Opposite from top: Bevis Bawa with friends including Vivien Leigh and Peter Finch; Lawrence Olivier arriving at Brief; Bevis Bawa with Donald Friend

Above from top: Pair of doors painted at Brief in 1958 by Donald Friend, displayed for many years by Geoffrey Bawa in his town house and now in the Art Gallery of New South Wales; *The Sick Mudaliyar* by Donald Friend (showing Bevis's friend Dr Raheem with a patient), painted in Aluthgama in 1958

Above from top: The gatepost at Brief, from the Diaries of Donald Friend; The gatepost at Brief, drawn by Rachel Sutherland; The gates of Brief, drawn by Channa Daswatte

Yesterday I worked on drawings of a design for two grand rococo gateposts, topped with figures, that Bevis is going to erect in the drive with a new front gate. He will make the figures himself, of concrete ... I am frequently called down for consultation, or 'to help with the beard' and invariably find a scene that recalls the enviable amateurs of a former age: at a convenient distance from the work in progress, (Bevis) lounges in a deckchair; pots of tea, plates of buns, cigarettes are near to hand. At the statue, one of the estate labourers, who has suddenly converted from rubber-tapping to plastering, stands with a trowel of cement waiting to be told where to apply it. 'Where', asks Bevis, 'do you think that trowel of cement should go?' 'On the big muscle of the arm.' 'But wouldn't that make it bulge too much?' 'Exaggerate always', says I.

Bevis accompanied Donald on tours to various parts of the island and he began to amass a huge collection of sketches of people and buildings, many of which found their way into a large mural, a sort of kaleidoscope panorama of Ceylon, which he painted on the verandah of the main house. As Bevis struggled to manage his estate, Donald looked on with detached amusement. That same year, he noted:

Poor Bevis! The last few days have been full of turmoil: the price of rubber, which has steadily been dropping in cents at a time, had another fall. Bevis worked on his accounts and found to his horror that the estate was now running at a loss of Rs. 700 per month, and immediately began an energetic drive to cut our costs. But, as is so typical of him, decided that they must be cut without reducing staff, for he has a most fatherly care of his workers.

And a month later:

Bevis has sold most of the estate and leased the rest of the rubber for a good price. He has kept only the house and garden and the twenty acre block on which my bungalow stands, at the same time arranging that his labourers will be re-employed by the new owner.

Through Bevis, Donald met the artist Barbara Sansoni and together they embarked on an experiment to manufacture decorated terracotta tiles. This effort was successful and they made large numbers of incised tiles which Donald and Bevis used in their garden installations. (Two panels of these tiles can still be seen on a verandah wall at Brief.) Sansoni later developed the technique further and produced a beautiful set of Stations of the Cross for Geoffrey Bawa's chapel at Bandarawela.

Donald Friend returned to Australia in 1962 but five years later moved to Bali, where he established himself as an artist and self-appointed feudal lord on the beach at Sanur, building a remarkable studio and surrounding it with guest pavilions and gardens. Here he struck up a friendship with an Indonesian impresario called Waworuntu who owned a beachside guest house. Friend helped Waworuntu transform it into the Tandjung Sari, the world's first tropical boutique hotel and it became an exclusive haunt of the super-rich and mega-famous. The hotel incorporated many features inspired by Friend's experiments with Bevis at Brief – friezes of decorated terracotta tiles, paving slabs decorated with the imprints of leaves, open-air bathrooms. Much imitated by architects and designers from across the tropical world, it was a key progenitor of what came to be known as 'Bali Style'. Later, in 1973, Friend invited Geoffrey Bawa to Bali and commissioned him to design an estate of fifteen exclusive villas at Batujimbar. This development, though never completed, was again hugely influential on later developments in tropical architecture.

Friend kept in touch with Bevis, and his diaries carry a sad postscript from 1973, when Bevis was facing the prospect of blindness with the onset of glaucoma:

After working in great calm and happiness ... came this letter from Bevis Bawa in Ceylon. So sad to see his handwriting, shaky and decrepit, and to read that his worst fears are being realised – the blindness that was coming on when I was last there. A wonderful, gentle, comical and delightful man.

My Dearest Donald,

Please do not think too badly of me for taking so long to write.

I've had your mural photographed in colour to be included in a series of Albums with an introduction by Robin Maugham. Your book filled me with delight and I did enjoy reading it. My eyes are rapidly going – when I go too I shall no longer have to depend on others. I hope that they will last some months because I hate leaving things in a mess.

With much love – I would like to give you more news but writing is a strain.

Bevis Bawa

JAMES BROUGHTON

In 1980 the California film-maker and poet James Broughton stayed at Brief for several weeks and wrote a poem as his mark of appreciation:

1
*In the land where the jaggery grows
and the skies are raucous with crows
years ago on a pastoral hill
(which was left to him in a will)
a young man was heard to declare:
'I will build my own kingdom there
and proclaim myself its chief
as the absolute Bawa of Brief.*

2
*I am much too bright and too tall
To dwell down upon the wastes
Where people are murky and small
Besides I have curious tastes
Which I wish to practice alone
And call my life my own
Time is a ruthless thief!'
Said the foolhardy Bawa of Brief.*

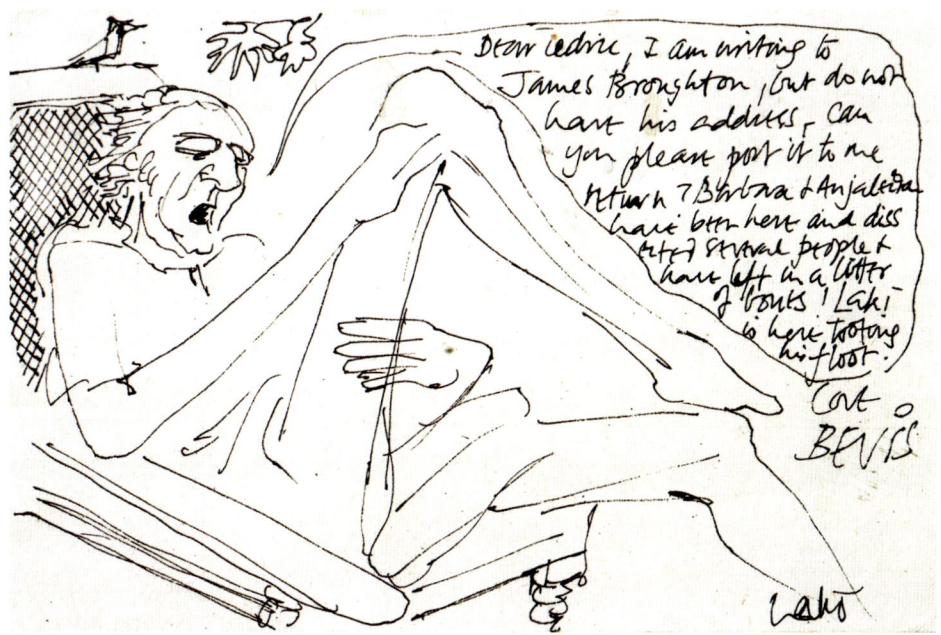

Left: A self-portrait by Bevis Bawa from the late 1980s.
Below: A postcard from Bevis Bawa to Cedric de Silva, drawn by Laki Senanayake

3
So he fashioned a baronial scene
of verdurous tropical green
with thickets and orchids and ponds
among highly exotic fronds,
tiled crannies of moss and fern
odd statues at every turn
and even a bold bas-relief
by the talented Bawa of Brief …

ROBIN MAUGHAM

The writer Robin Maugham, nephew of Somerset Maugham, dropped in one day in 1974 on his way down south on an unsuccessful bid to buy Count de Mauny's Taprobane Island. In his Handbook for the Ceylon Traveller from the same year, he wrote:

On the way to Taprobane we spent the night at one of the most famous houses in the Orient which was built by a gentle giant of a man called Bevis Bawa whom I had known for many years. Bevis had found his Nirvana; indeed he created it.

The house is a fantastic series of rambling courtyards, patios, loggias and terraces and is filled with furniture – old and new, indigenous and exotic – all blending together to make it one of the loveliest houses in the East, adorned with paintings and antiques which Bevis has found during his wanderings around the world.

The harmony of the garden at 'Brief' is unexpected because, as Bevis explains it, it consists of several small gardens – thought out by him in various moods and at various times during its growth over the last forty years. The result is a climax of loveliness, a proclamation that nature can triumph over the hideous inventions of mankind.

In the leafy trees and shrubs the wild birds call and sing. Flowers glitter in the sunshine. Gracefully shaped vistas reach out towards the horizon. Tranquillity pervades the green terraces. Peace covers the house with a soft cloak. Peace falls over the lawns like a blessing. Peace is everywhere. For this is a Paradise, made by the sensibility of one man, created by his patience and love.

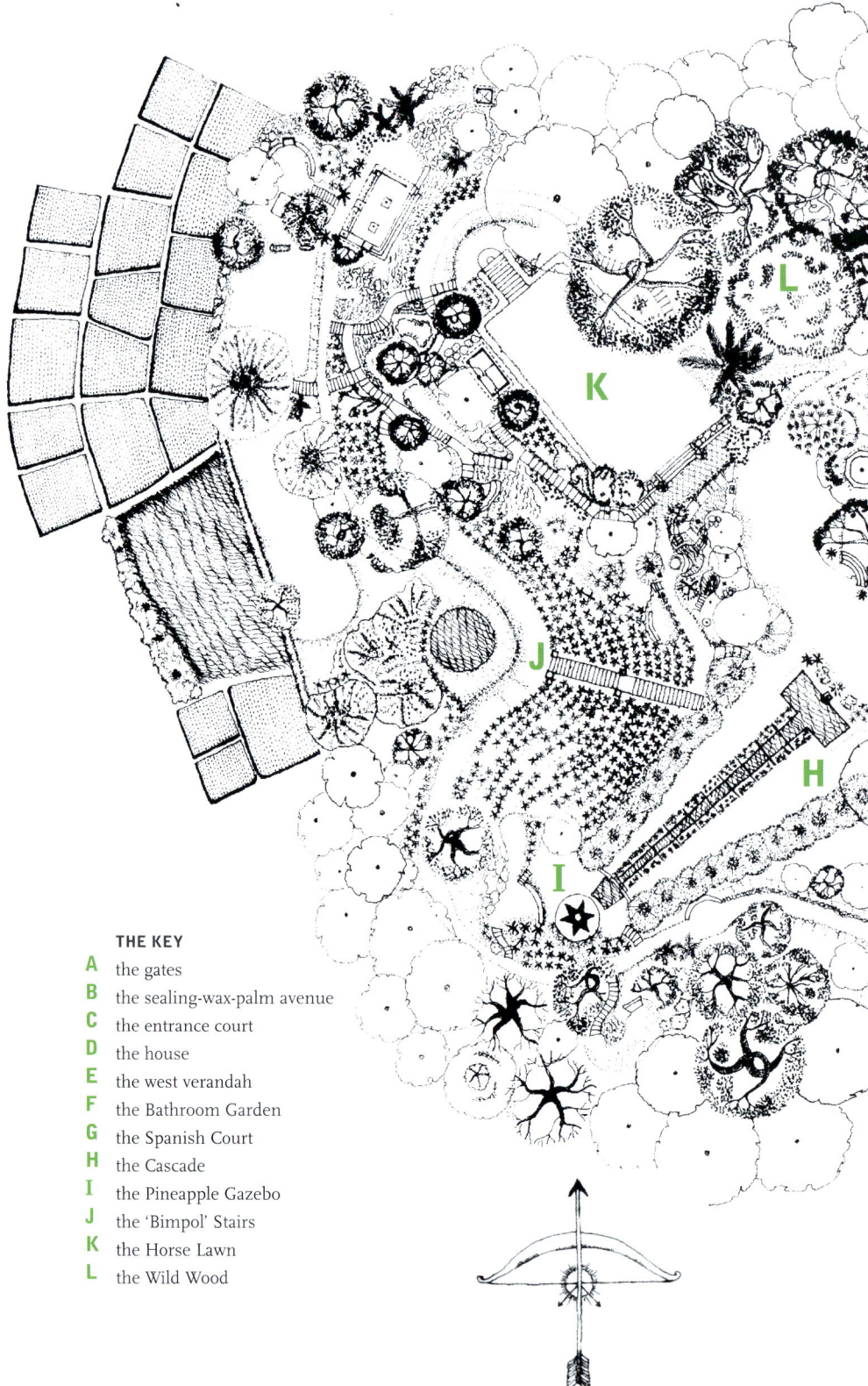

THE KEY

A the gates
B the sealing-wax-palm avenue
C the entrance court
D the house
E the west verandah
F the Bathroom Garden
G the Spanish Court
H the Cascade
I the Pineapple Gazebo
J the 'Bimpol' Stairs
K the Horse Lawn
L the Wild Wood

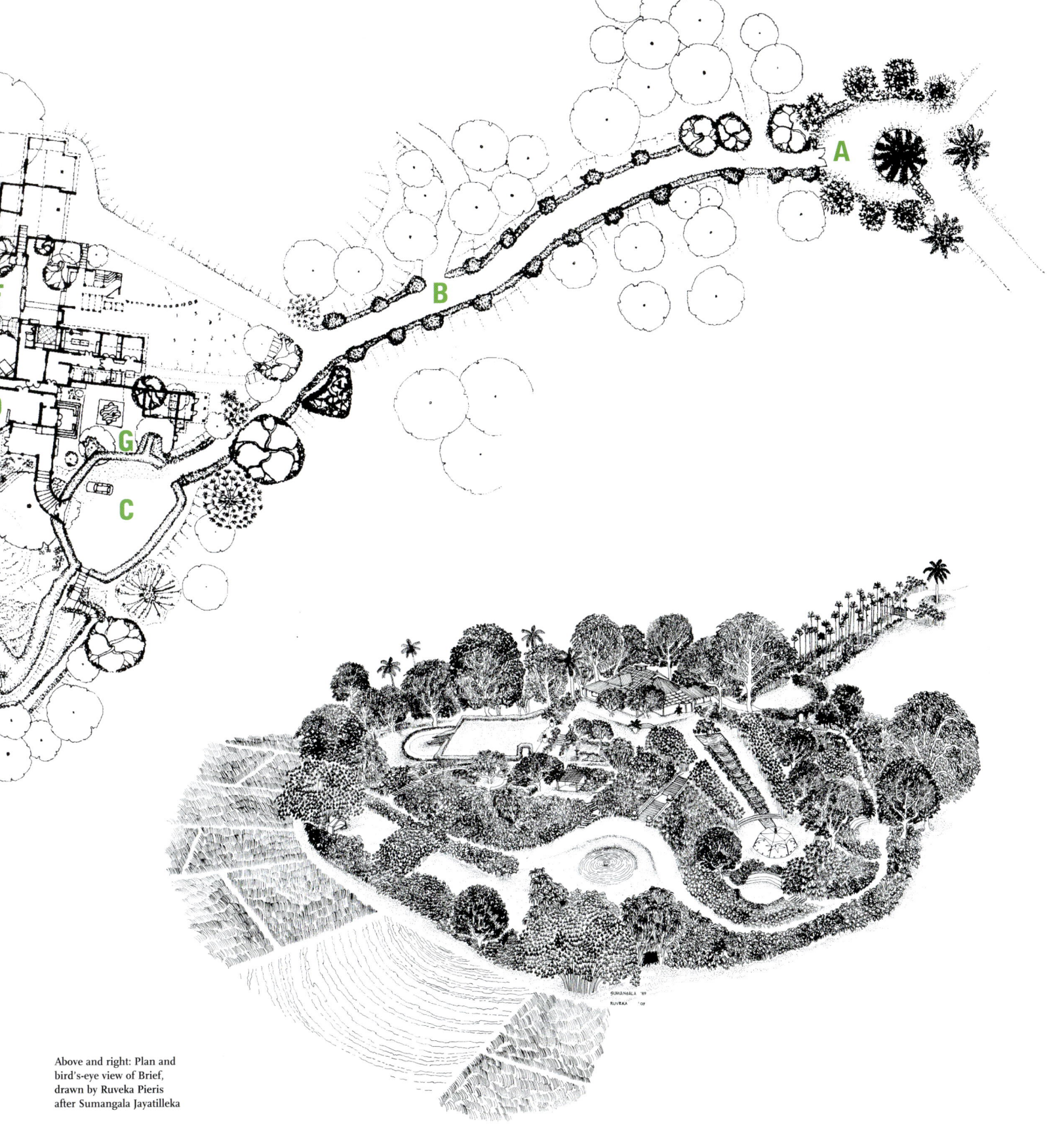

Above and right: Plan and bird's-eye view of Brief, drawn by Ruveka Pieris after Sumangala Jayatilleka

III Brief

The road to Brief strikes inland from the coast, skirting the north bank of the Bentota River to arrive in Darga Town, a predominantly Muslim community marked by a cluster of modern mosques, and then crosses a large, flat landscape of marshland and paddy studded with small tree-clad hills. After numerous false trails and confusions, the determined visitor will arrive at a tree-lined circus where the gates of Brief stand between their ornate rococo gateposts. From here a curving avenue of red-barked sealing-wax palms climbs gently up to a second circus, seemingly carved out from a dense stand of bamboo, where a large bell hangs before a small black-and-white door set in a samara-coloured wall. This blank and enclosed entrance space conveys a strange sense of mystery and anticipation, and the small hole in the wall appears like a door in Alice's Wonderland.

Pages 50–51: The avenue of sealing-wax palms

Opposite: Detail from Donald Friend's mural showing Bevis Bawa before the gates of Brief

the entrance Above: Gatepost made in 1957 by Bevis Bawa and Donald Friend; the entrance to the house and garden behind a curtain of white bourgainvillea

The door opens not into the garden but directly on to a curving staircase which rises past the statue of a boy balancing a large seashell on his head into the main bungalow, arriving at a verandah next to Donald Friend's now flaking panoramic mural of Sri Lanka. Here Bevis Bawa sits in his planter's chair before the gates of Brief while the whole panoply of Sri Lankan life swirls around him: a sensational painting in a sensational setting.

the main house   Opposite: The stairs up from the entrance with the boy carrying the sea-shell lamp-holder

Above: The south verandah with a table etched by Donald Friend

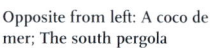

Opposite from left: A coco de mer; The south pergola

The bungalow grew over time from its original core of cellular rooms and is now encased within a cordon of verandahs and courtyards. The more public and open parts of the garden fan out from the main verandahs down the hillside towards the west, while the north- and east-facing sides open into a private world of pool courts and shady loggias. Within the bungalow are the remains of Bevis's extensive collections of art and furniture: an aluminium sculpture by Donald Friend, panels of terracotta tiles fashioned by Friend with Barbara Sansoni, paintings and drawings by Laki Senanayake.

the main house Above and right: Views of the main sitting room

west of the house   Above from top left: The south-west corner of the house; Towards the cascade from the west verandah; View along the west verandah with a red ginger

Opposite from top: Window in the west verandah; Towards the Horse Lawn from the west verandah

Page 62: From top left: Mosaic table; Congia; Shadow patterns; Black lily

Page 63: From top left: Song of India; Leaf pattern in a cement table top by Bevis Bawa; red ginger; Patterned tiles by Donald Friend and Barbara Sansoni

III Brief 61

To the east the main verandah is separated from a private garden court by an intriguing screen made up of glass bottles which offers a blurred image of a shower cubicle beyond. From here a series of small courtyards connect to what in former times was a guest pavilion located above the main garage. This area is dotted with playful sculptures now almost hidden from view by the all-enveloping vegetation.

Right: The 'Pissing Boy' shower by Bevis Bawa. The bottle wall was made by Barbara Sansoni

66 III Brief north of the house Above: The west wall of the Bathroom Garden with the Moon Gate. The urns were made to a design by Donald Friend

'I've joined in partnership with Bevis to design layouts and decorations for the refurbishing of Bentota Rest House, which (involves) designing urns and simple bas relief motifs. It's all rather fun. The garage workshop at Brief is once again a scene of great activity with workers casting great garden urns and seats from concrete moulds.' DONALD FRIEND, 1957

north of the house   Above and opposite: Sculpted heads by Bevis Bawa and Donald Friend

On the other side of the bungalow is a private world of secret courtyards. To the south a small walled garden focuses on a mirror pool set within a white surround. On one side a Christ-like figure hangs on the wall, while on the other an image of a sleeping boy is etched into a stone bench. Ahead a statue in a niche nods to a smaller court which serves as an outdoor bathroom and is dominated by a giant gargoyle sculpted by Bevis as a caricature of Donald Friend.

east of the house   Opposite: Views and details of the Spanish Court

Right from top: Figure of a boy etched into a bench by Donald Friend; Leaf pattern on concrete floor tile

'The courtyard is furnished with large pots of terracotta or rough Chinese glazed pottery, containing various exotic plants. In the centre of the little lawn, a fountain, and at the furthest end from my room, an open-air shower room furnished with stone benches and plants, a black glass mirror set in one wall, and a fountain with a grotesque head that spouts water.' DONALD FRIEND, 1957

east of the house   Above: View from the Spanish Court into the Gargoyle Court

Opposite from top: The Gargoyle Bath – a caricature of Donald Friend by Bevis Bawa; Sculpture by Bevis Bawa

The main gardens are laid out around three main prongs. The first of these takes the form of a sloping corridor formed by thick clumps of bamboos. At the top a young boy framed within a small alcove pours water from an urn into a pool from which it flows down in a cascade of stepped basins. These are reminiscent of Vignola's cascades at the Villa Lante and the casino garden at Caprarola which Bevis had visited during his Italian tour in 1949. The cascade terminates in a grass circus, at the centre of which is a gazebo in the form of a hexagonal metal tent crowned by a pineapple.

Page 74: From top left: Pink striped trumpet lily; Stamens of a pink striped trumpet lily; Looking up the Cascade towards the house; Looking down the Cascade towards the Pineapple Gazebo

Page 75: From top: The head of the Cascade; Pink striped trumpet lily; The Pineapple Gazebo

The second prong branches off on the right from the cascade and descends via a steep flight of steps to a circular pool surrounded by giant bamboos and a type of fern to which Bevis gave the name 'bimpol' (dwarf coconut).

south-west of the house   Opposite from top left: Around the 'Bimpol' Stairs and Circular Pond; Leaves of the heliconia and philodendron plants

Above: The Circular Pond at the foot of the 'Bimpol' Stairs

The third prong begins with a large square lawn surrounded by a hedge from which a short flight of steps drops down into a 'moon-stone court'. From here a tunnel plunges off on the right into a hidden section of the garden called 'the forest' which has been left to grow wild.

north-west of the house   Above and opposite: The Horse Lawn

Page 80: From top: The Wild Wood; *Alpinia abundiflora*

Page 81: From top: *Alpinia Abundiflora*; Broken urns by Donald Friend beside the path in the Wild Wood; The Wild Wood

west of the house Above: The Japanese Garden

Opposite from left: A stone pagoda; The bird bath – 'The Boy with a Clam Shell'

Pages 84–5: A stone urn nestling in the vegetation

The three prongs are connected by a series of pathways which thread through the surrounding forest. Here the wanderer may chance upon a small Japanese garden, a carved-stone basin fed from the mouth of a turtle, a pavilion designed for alfresco dining, and half a dozen other small clearings. Small gaps in the thick vegetation offer continually varying glimpses of the surrounding paddy fields or of neighbouring woodland.

west of the house   Opposite and above left: Pathways around the west of the house.
From top left: Lamp-holder in the Picnic Pavilion; The Turtle Fountain; Detail

'Trees do not hate. Their very stance is elegant and beautiful to watch. Though man delights in destroying plant life, I have never known plants to let down man ... My gardens have now reached the end of their progress and they now rest in peace – perhaps looking back with happiness on their past, perhaps sad that they can no longer move on to further changes of mood.' BEVIS BAWA, 1974

west of the house Opposite and above: Pathways in the lower garden

Pages 90–91: Canopy of trees and climbing vegetation in the lower garden

IV
Lunuganga

'I love this country and I must find a site where I would be happy, preferably near a river or a lake. If I can't find one here then I shall have to comb the earth until I do.' GEOFFREY BAWA, 1989

After his mother's death in April 1946, Geoffrey Bawa decided to quit Ceylon, ostensibly for good. In quick succession he sold his half of the family home in Darley Road and his own house in Torrington Avenue, as well as some coconut estates which he had inherited. In January 1947, having entrusted his precious Rolls Royce to his brother, he boarded a Norwegian schooner which carried him eastwards to Penang and Singapore, and thence to the United States, where he spent the next six months. In Los Angeles he befriended a young film actor called Victor Chapin, and they drove together across the continent to New York and down to Miami. In the autumn of 1947 the two men sailed for England, where Geoffrey met up briefly with old Cambridge friends before crossing the Channel to visit Georgette Camille in Paris. At the end of the year Geoffrey and Victor travelled down to Italy, where Geoffrey rented a house overlooking Lake Garda, not far from the home of Guy Strutt's aunt at Cola di Lazise, while Victor went to Rome to work on a film.

Geoffrey was returning to the country which he would later profess to love above all others. Acting on a whim, he decided to settle there permanently and resolved to buy the house he was renting and transform it into a classical villa surrounded by gardens. But his plans started to unravel when he discovered that buying a property in Italy was fraught with bureaucratic obstacles and that his Ceylon savings amounted to less than he had imagined. After months spent battling unsuccessfully with Italian lawyers, he conceded defeat and, in July 1948, boarded a ship that would take him back to Ceylon.

Ceylon had regained its independence that February, and Geoffrey's return could be construed as that of a prodigal son renewing his ties to his native land. But his brother, Bevis, later recalled that Geoffrey had already booked his return passage to Europe and only intended to stay for six weeks. Geoffrey had clearly arrived at a crossroads: he was in his thirtieth year, he was qualified in a profession he hated, and he lacked any sense of purpose or direction. Although of mixed parentage, he was conscious of his Asian origins but, having spent a third of his life abroad, had developed a European outlook. Now homeless, he had to presume on his brother's hospitality. Bevis was still acting as aide-de-camp to the British governor and dividing his time between his official duties in Colombo and his growing landscaping business at Brief. He invited Geoffrey to install himself in the estate bungalow and to stay for as long as he wanted.

The rubber estate at Brief was ailing, and by this time Bevis had already started to sell off chunks to neighbours. However, as the estate had shrunk, the gardens around the bungalow had grown, both in size and in beauty. Bevis had been working on them intensively for six years, and they had reached their full extent, covering an area of about 2.5 hectares. Geoffrey saw Brief at close quarters for the first time: he was enchanted by the gardens and impressed by what his brother had achieved. When Bevis suggested that his

Opposite: Looking north-west across Dedduwa Lake

Above from top: The bungalow in 1948; The north-west verandah; An early version of the entrance steps; Outside the Roman Pavilion

brother buy a similar property and settle down permanently in Ceylon, he responded positively. As Bevis put it in his unpublished memoir:

On Geoffrey's return home (in 1948) I told him I envied his travels. 'But you don't realise', said he, 'that you have a home of your own, and I have not. I love this country and I must find a site where I would be happy, preferably near a river or a lake. If I can't find one here then I shall have to comb the earth until I do.' Geoffrey had already booked his passage back to Europe and we had only four weeks to find such a spot. After three weeks of fruitless search we were sitting at the Bentota Rest House, trying to drown our depression, when the local Excise Inspector joined us for a drink. As we told him our sad story his flushed red face beamed and he said: 'Did you think of that bungalow on the hillock overlooking the Dedduwa Lake which the District Revenue Officer rents? It's not much more than a mile inland from where we're sitting, and the owner, who lives here in Bentota, is keen to sell.'

Geoffrey rushed off at once to see the bungalow in question and found a dilapidated building in the middle of a small rubber estate of about 7 hectares. The estate occupied a narrow strip of land, about 400 metres in length, which straddled a promontory on the further eastern side of the brackish lagoon known as Dedduwa Lake. It spanned between the northern and southern halves of the lake, rising and falling across two low hills. The bungalow, a gloomy structure engulfed by rubber trees, occupied the summit of the northern hill and enjoyed restricted views across the northern half of the lake. It would be a simple matter to clear away the trees and open up the northern view, but Geoffrey also understood that a corresponding view towards the south was waiting to be discovered. This was the piece of land for which he had been searching, and he resolved to buy it immediately.

The principal owner was a widow, but, as was often the case in Ceylon, there were many other sub-owners whose agreement was needed to enable the sale, and a new house had to be found for the Revenue Officer. In time all of this was achieved, and Geoffrey, abandoning his plans for further travel, became the proud owner of a country estate which he named 'Lunuganga', or Salt River.

DESIGN AND INSPIRATION

Geoffrey never sat down and drew up a master plan for the garden: each move was simply a response to what was there, to the 'spirit of the place'. Directly inspired by the experience of staying at Brief, he was determined to outshine his brother and make a garden that would be distinctly different.

It is sometimes assumed that, following his aborted plan to buy a villa in Italy, Geoffrey's inspiration for Lunuganga was drawn from his time there and that one of his aims was to produce a tropical version of the garden he had hoped to create beside Lake Garda. There is little evidence on the ground to support this. He had been bowled over by the gardens he had seen in Italy – particularly the Giardino dei Giusti at Verona and Vignola's gardens at the Villa Lante and at Caprarola – but while these helped to awaken his interest in garden design, they had little direct influence on the planning of Lunuganga. The one Italian garden that perhaps did leave its mark was the Villa Lante's strange neighbour, the *sacro bosco* of the Villa Orsini near Bomarzo, a naturalistic garden studded with grotesque sculptures.

In fact English landscape gardens of the eighteenth century such as Stowe and Stourhead appear to have exerted a much more tangible influence on Geoffrey's ideas. He had very happy memories of his time at Cambridge and of staying with friends in the country. It was through them that he came to appreciate the subtleties of the garden planning of William Kent and his contemporaries.

Geoffrey had inherited a love of travel from his mother, and hardly a year passed without his embarking on at least one foreign journey. He travelled widely and visited gardens on every continent, though he rarely used a camera, storing his impressions within his encyclopaedic memory. He retained a vivid impression of the walled gardens of Suzhou in China, which he had visited with his mother as a teenager, and in later years came to admire the Moghul gardens of North India and the courtyards of the Alhambra in Granada.

He owned a considerable library of books – many of them, according to his brother, 'borrowed' from friends – but relatively few were on garden design. One of his favourites was Sir George Sitwell's *On the Making of Gardens*, which had first appeared in 1909 and which was reprinted in 1949 with illustrations by John Piper. Sitwell extolled the virtues of the Italian garden, singling out the villas d'Este and Lante for highest praise. He was extremely critical of the rigidity of French Renaissance gardens but also mocked the faux naturalism of 'Capability' Brown, and many of his ideas accorded with Geoffrey's own. Geoffrey also admired J. C. Shepherd and G. A. Jellicoe's *Italian Gardens of the Renaissance* (1925) and acquired Georgina Masson's *Italian Gardens* when it appeared in 1961. He also consulted H. F. Macmillan's *Tropical Planting and Gardening with Special Reference to Ceylon*, which had appeared in 1931.

But Lunuganga also speaks to that long tradition of Sri Lankan garden- and landscape-making which Geoffrey had had ample opportunity to explore during his island-wide travels: the bizarre boulder gardens of the first Buddhist ascetics; the rolling park landscapes of the Anuradhapura monasteries; the pleasure gardens of the Sinhalese kings; the mysterious retreats of the forest hermits; the vivid green mosaics of rice paddy; the lines of leaning rubber trees and gently swaying coconut palms; the neatly hedged lawns of the estate-bungalow gardens. This tradition had a profound influence on his designs for buildings such as the Polontalawa Estate Bungalow (1964), the Ruhunu University Campus (1984) and the Kandalama Hotel (1992), but it also influenced him in the making of his own garden.

A final analysis suggests that Lunuganga is a unique creation which combines memories

Above, clockwise from top left: The cascade at Villa Lante; Two views of Stourhead in Wiltshire; Giardino dei Giusti, Verona; Two sculptures at Villa Orsini, Bomarzo; the Alhambra at Granada

Above from top: The North Terrace in 1952, showing Elinor Williams, Jane Keen, Geoffrey Bawa and Arthur van Langenburg; Georgette Camille and Victor Chapin, January 1949, on the verandah; Geoffrey Bawa's Rolls Royce, 1949

of a thousand and one experiences, a landscape that fuses European and Asian traditions of garden-making, a place that, as Vicino Orsini said of his sacro bosco at Bomarzo, 'resembles itself and nothing else'.

The challenge of the garden project awakened Geoffrey's latent interest in architecture. Although he didn't want for ideas, he soon discovered that he lacked the technical skills to bring them about. Among the first visitors to Lunuganga were his cousin Georgette Camille and his American friend Victor Chapin. They arrived at the end of 1948 before the house was ready and stayed initially at Brief with Bevis. Georgette was surprised that Geoffrey was lavishing so much money on the project and urged him to become an architect 'so that you can use other people's money to develop your ideas'. In 1954 he returned to Britain to study architecture, qualifying in 1957 at the age of thirty-eight. Back in Colombo, he joined the firm of Edwards, Reid and Begg, starting a career that would span four decades and make him one of the most respected and influential Asian architects of his generation. But that is another story.

A FIFTY-YEAR GARDEN

Geoffrey Bawa devoted most of his free time – nearly every weekend when he was in Sri Lanka – to his garden, which continued to develop over a period of fifty years, each stage of evolution reflecting Geoffrey's current preoccupations. He never kept a record of its progress, and it is now difficult to unravel its precise chronology.

During the early 1950s, trees were cleared from the north terrace to open up the view towards the lake and the nearby island. The entrance porch on the west front was turned into a verandah, and beside it two aralia (frangipani) trees were planted and trained to form a sinuous sculpture of gnarled trunks. The drive, meanwhile, was diverted towards a lower terrace below the south-east corner of the bungalow, whence a sculptural cascade of steps led up to a new entrance on the south front.

Work then began on clearing the southern hill, which later took on the name 'Cinnamon Hill' in memory of the cinnamon plantation which had existed before the rubber trees. Trees were cut and earth removed to create a layered view from the south front of the house, taking in the summit of the hill, a sliver of lake and a fringe of distant hills crowned by the happy accident of a brilliant white dagoba. A single moonamal tree was left to mark the summit of Cinnamon Hill, and a large Chinese pot was placed beneath its branches. The gaze of a visitor arriving on the south terrace was now channelled through a cone of space created by the flanking woods and deflected upwards by the urn and over Cinnamon Hill towards the distant dagoba and the sky. The estate road that ran in the dip at the foot of Cinnamon Hill towards a neighbouring property was now hidden within an almost subterranean ha-ha, and the two halves of the garden were linked by a covered 'bridge of sighs'.

While the woods were being cleared to the south, the gentle northern slopes of the main hill were cut away in order to create an artificial cliff below the northern terrace. This was then criss-crossed with staircases and ramps which, to honour Geoffrey's friend and then colleague Ulrik Plesner, were named the 'Scala Danesi', or 'Danish Steps'. The area immediately below the cliff was raised slightly above flood level to create a long transverse promenade called the 'Broad Walk' which was marked by an avenue of plumerias. The swathe of land to the north of this was then turned into a chequerboard pattern of rice squares, and beyond this a water garden was established along the side of the lake.

The house itself meanwhile had been cocooned within a carapace of walls to form a transitional zone of private courtyards and verandahs between the interior rooms and the garden. Thus Geoffrey's own suite of rooms now opened onto two separate courtyards: the bedroom connected with an austere paved court with a rectangular reflecting pool which, in turn, linked to a loggia overlooking the western lawns, while the bathroom connected to an outer bathroom courtyard which contained, as well as a shower and plunge pool, its own private lookout tower.

But the interior of the house was used only for sleeping, and life at Lunuganga focused mainly on the garden: Geoffrey once declared that he had not eaten in the dining room on more than half a dozen occasions, and nobody ever sat in the sitting room. Meals were served in different corners of the garden according to time of day and weather: breakfast might be served on the South Terrace, lunch on the far edge of the Eastern Terrace, dinner on the main verandah next to the big frangipani, and evening drinks on the western lawns.

In 1970 a new left-wing government seemed to threaten both the future of Geoffrey's architectural practice and his unique way of life. For a time he even toyed with the idea of moving both office and home to India. During the 1960s he had leased an area of paddy below the western terraces from his neighbour and had acquired both the large island to the north of the peninsula and a smaller island off its western tip. The total area of the estate now exceeded 10 hectares. When the new government introduced measures to nationalize all large land holdings, Lunuganga came under threat. Prime Minister Srimavo Bandaranayake had protected her own land from the legislation by declaring it a nature reserve, so Geoffrey, following her example, registered the larger island as a bird sanctuary. This was a time of great austerity, and he decided to establish a small farm on part of the garden, both to ward off possible takeover and to supply much-needed milk and eggs. New chicken and cow sheds were built at the eastern end of the hill, and cows replaced peacocks on the terraces.

Following a further change of government in 1977, Geoffrey received commissions to build a new parliament at Kotte on the eastern outskirts of Colombo and a new university at Matara in southern Sri Lanka, and embarked on the busiest decade of his career. Lunuganga became an important refuge for him and a place where he could work in peace on new designs. He now converted the cow sheds into a gallery and built a small guesthouse next to the ha-ha so that staff could come and work with him at weekends. In 1983 he added a studio on the edge of the Eastern Terrace and named it 'Sandela'. This elegant pavilion incorporated doors and windows which had been salvaged from demolitions and took on an immediate patina of age. Geoffrey delighted to recount how a group of Japanese visitors admired the newly completed pavilion: 'So ancient, so beautiful – how old Mr Bawa?' The various pavilions which he added to the garden often reflected ideas and aesthetics that he was developing for projects in the office: thus a pump house next to the gallery, known affectionately as the 'Hen House', seems to précis the design of the parliament at Kotte.

After 1976, Geoffrey developed a close friendship with the London-based architects Christoph Bon and Joe Chamberlin and Joe's wife Jean, all members of Chamberlin, Powell & Bon, the designers of the London Barbican. When Joe died suddenly in 1979, Geoffrey was drawn in by Christoph and Jean to fill the empty place in their triangle. From then on, he was able to treat their London home as his own, and they were regular visitors to Lunuganga. Another friend of the 1980s was the young architect C. Anjalendran, who acted as Geoffrey's self-appointed amanuensis and often helped him with his garden projects. In 1986 the four joined forces to put together a monograph on Geoffrey's work. Produced by Mimar in Singapore and edited by Brian Brace Taylor, this carried the first published account of Lunuganga. Then in 1990 Christoph Bon collaborated with a young photographer called Dominic Sansoni to produce a book devoted exclusively to the garden. *Lunuganga*, published by Times Editions in Singapore and

Above from top: Geoffrey Bawa with Dr Raheem and Jean Chamberlin on the Eastern Terrace, *c.* 1990; Jean Chamberlin with Geoffrey Bawa on the West Verandah, *c.* 1985; Geoffrey Bawa with Michael Ondaatje in the garden Bajaj (motor trishaw)

an evocative study in black-and-white, was surely one of the most beautiful garden books of all time.

At the end of the 1980s Geoffrey withdrew from the busy practice which he had headed for thirty years and started a new studio-office in his Colombo home. He now had more time for foreign travel and more time to spend in his Lunuganga garden. In 1991 the new office landed the commission to build the astonishing Kandalama Hotel near Dambulla in Sri Lanka's dry zone, and Geoffrey marked this moment with a new guest pavilion on the far side of Cinnamon Hill, the design of which seems to paraphrase the emerging design of the hotel.

The large leather-bound visitors' book with its signed comments, sketches and pasted-in photographs provides a graphic history of the garden: in 1957 Donald Friend calls to pay his respects and leaves a centaur on the page; in 1966 Ismeth Raheem records having seen forty species of bird in one afternoon; in 1973 Donald flies in from Bali to discuss the designs for his Batujimbar muesum and leaves a doodle; in 1997 President Chandrika Kumaratunga approves the design for her new residence; in 1998 the Prince of Wales invites himself to tea.

Of all the visitors to Lunuganga, the most unexpected was the Sri Lankan inventor Ray Wijewardene, who crash-landed his micro-light aeroplane on the roof of the main bungalow in 1988. He described this surprising event in a letter:

I circled the house to set up my approach, and then came in low over the lake. I managed to clear the ridge of the house, but then a branch of the araliya tree caught my under-carriage, and I flopped down, somewhat heavily, on the ridge.

GB appeared from below and called up: 'Ray – are you alright?' I took a moment to recover myself and shouted down: 'I'm fine, but I'm sorry to have made such an awkward entrance. There are quite a few broken tiles up here.' GB called back: 'Don't worry about those – have you damaged the tree?' I glanced back at the leaves and branches scattered among the broken tiles and sadly advised him: 'I'm awfully sorry, Geoff, but I seem to have broken some branches too.' He studied the situation: 'Don't worry one bit: it needed pruning! What shall we do now?' I said: 'I seem to recall that you invited us for lunch.' He laughed and said: 'Yes, I did ask you to drop in, but I didn't expect you to take me so literally.'

The Cinnamon Hill House was the last new addition to the garden, and in February 1998 Geoffrey entertained his last distinguished visitor. Prince Charles, in Sri Lanka to attend the celebrations marking the fiftieth anniversary of independence, slipped away from the parades and drove down from Colombo for a guided tour of Lunuganga.

A few weeks later, Geoffrey suffered a serious stroke which left him paralyzed and unable to speak, and it seemed that the story of Lunuganga would draw to its close. In fact, he lived on for

Opposite from top: A sketch from the Visitors' Book by Laki Senanayake; A page from the Visitors' Book from 1973 showing a self-portrait by Donald Friend and an aerial view of the garden; A sketch from the Visitors' Book. Opposite bottom from left: Geoffrey Bawa showing the Visitors' Book to the Raheem family, September 1997; A photograph in the Visitors' Book commemorating the visit of Prince Charles in February 1998

Left: A sketch from the Visitors' Book by Rachel Sutherland. Below from left: Aerial view of Lunuganga in 2004; Garden staff at work

a further five years, and though his care regime dictated that he should spend most of his time in Colombo, he made regular visits to the garden. His office was now run by a young architect called Channa Daswatte who had been his associate for a number of years, while his estate was managed by a trust formed by a group of his friends. Day-to-day management of the garden was entrusted to two young architects, Michael Daniels and Asha de Silva. When Geoffrey stayed at Lunuganga, he would join Michael and Asha in his wheelchair each morning and participate in the daily maintenance of the garden: Michael would point to a tree or bush and Geoffrey would direct the pruning by squeezing Asha's hand.

Lunuganga functioned for Bawa as a distant retreat, an outpost on the edge of the known world, challenging the infinite horizon of the ocean to the west and the endless switchback of hills to the east, reducing an open landscape to a series of outdoor rooms, a civilized garden within the larger garden of Sri Lanka. Today it seems so natural, so established, that it is difficult to appreciate how much effort went into its creation. Nor is it apparent just how much maintenance work is needed to achieve such a precise level of careful casualness. Ignore the garden for a week and the pathways and staircases will clog up with leaves, after a month the lawns will run wild, within a year the terraces will crumble, and soon the jungle will return.

Geoffrey Bawa died in 2003 and was cremated in a moving ceremony on the summit of Cinnamon Hill. His ashes were scattered at the heart of the garden to which he had devoted so much time, energy and devotion.

During his final years as he sat on the terrace and watched the sun going down across the lake he must have wondered what would become of the magic world that he had created. Should it become a national monument patrolled by security guards or a country club for rich Colombo-ites? Better to abandon it and let the jungle creep back!

Many monsoons have blown their course since Geoffrey was struck down by illness, but, miraculously, the garden has survived, still watched over by the Lunuganga Trust and lovingly cared for by Michael and Asha. Visitors are admitted on most days in small supervised groups, and the various pavilions serve as the guest suites of a unique country hotel. Lunuganga now hosts cultural events and welcomes resident artists from around the world. Geoffrey Bawa would have nodded his approval.

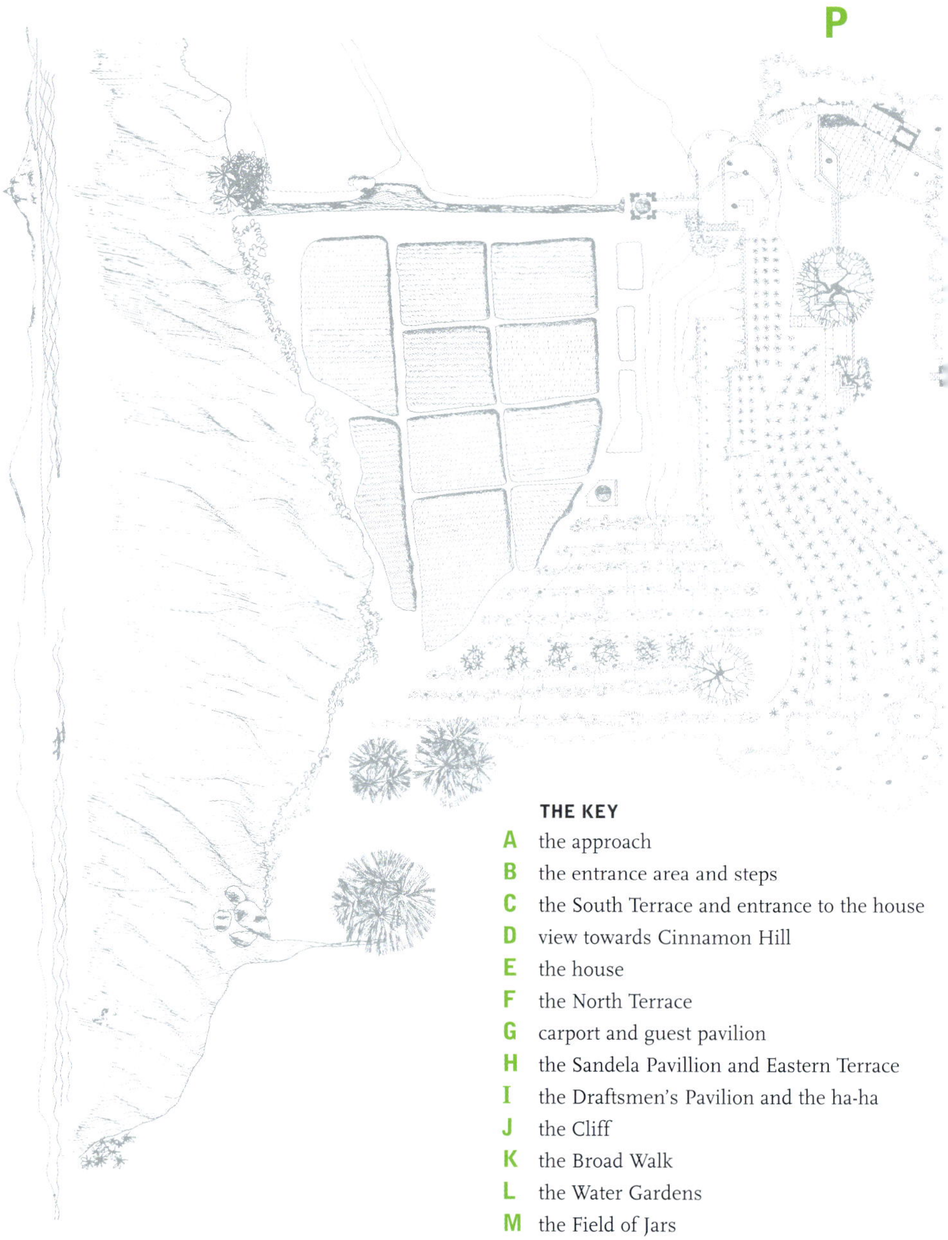

THE KEY

- **A** the approach
- **B** the entrance area and steps
- **C** the South Terrace and entrance to the house
- **D** view towards Cinnamon Hill
- **E** the house
- **F** the North Terrace
- **G** carport and guest pavilion
- **H** the Sandela Pavillion and Eastern Terrace
- **I** the Draftsmen's Pavilion and the ha-ha
- **J** the Cliff
- **K** the Broad Walk
- **L** the Water Gardens
- **M** the Field of Jars
- **N** the Western Terrace
- **O** Cinnamon Hill
- **P** site of Cinnamon Hill House

Left: Geoffrey Bawa with a gardener, c. 1989. Above: Plan of Lunuganga in 1985 by an unknown draftsman

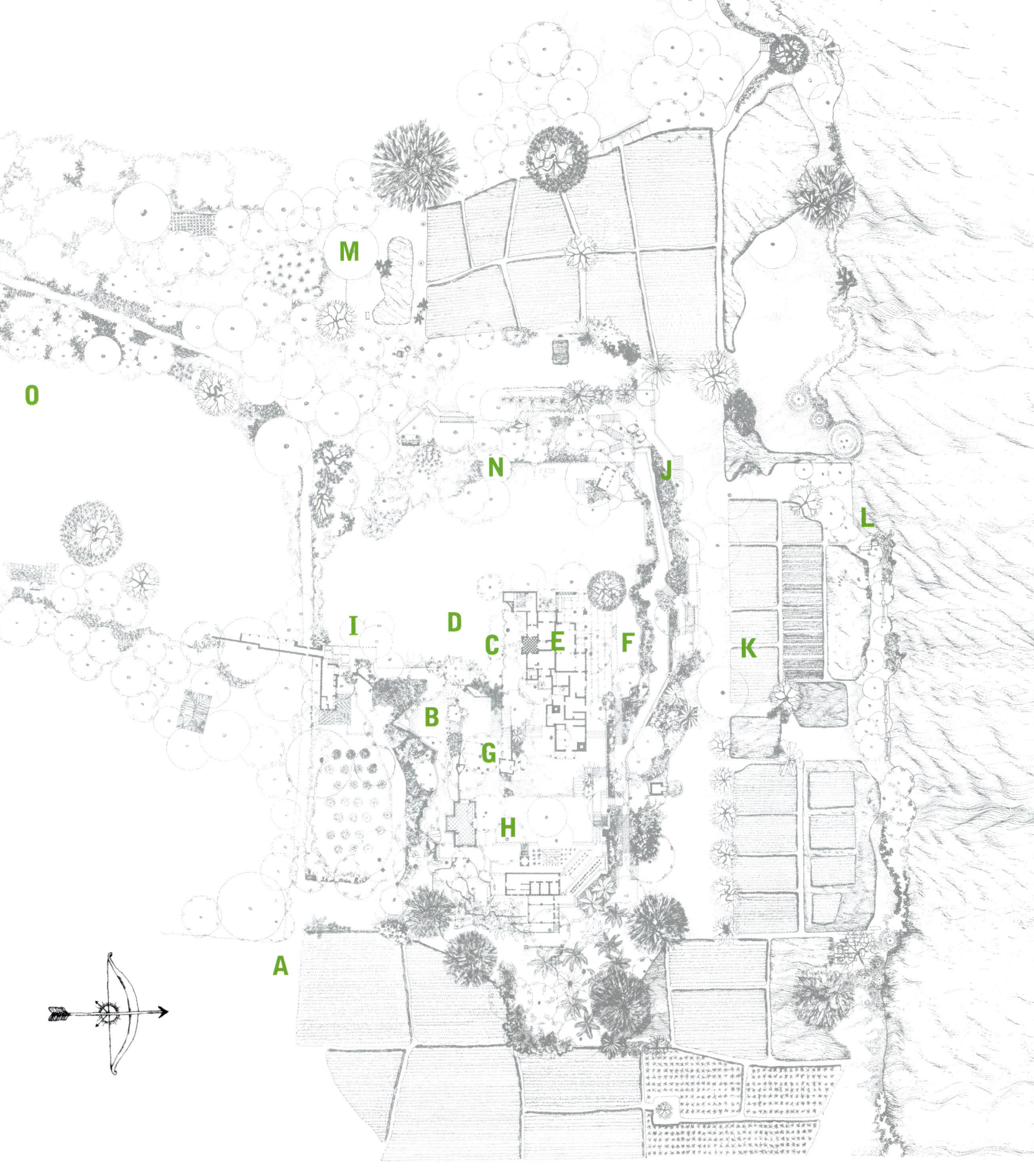

'The planting in the village and surrounding lands is lush and overwhelmingly green – monochromatic but with infinite variety – the earth seldom evident except when the rice fields are tilled and the dark brown is set beautifully against the green lines of the dividing bunds to form elegant geometric man-made patterns. There is no winter in Sri Lanka – only monsoons change the mood and light. The landscape is large in scale and the small village houses disappear behind foliage, the greatest beauty being the effect of the sunlight filtering through the leaves. There are hardly any flowers, except for wild hibiscus, ipomea, jasmine, mugerin and alamanda – all casually planted and giving an occasional pointilistic moment of varied colour against the green background. Lunuganga from the start was to be an extension of the surroundings – a garden within a larger garden.' GEOFFREY BAWA, 1990

the entrance   Pages 102–3: The obelisk gatepost at the entrance to the garage court
Opposite: Base of a tree

After leaving the busy main Galle road at Bentota, a small bumpy lane leads through a labyrinth of small villages along a causeway that crosses the neck of Dedduwa Lake and eventually arrives at the gates of Lunuganga. After much ringing of bells, the gates open to a steep gravel path which leads up to the tiered entrance court and the cascade of steps which ascend to the south front of the house.

the entrance Opposite from top left: The outer entrance gate; Early morning light; Looking back towards the driveway from the carport
Above: Looking from the carport towards the entrance steps

The house occupies the conceptual centre of the garden and serves both to connect and separate its different parts. To the north the main lawn runs to the edge of the cliff and offers views down towards the Broad Walk and the Water Gardens; to the east a series of gravel terraces step down past the Sandela to the Gothic Court and the Gallery; to the south the lawn sweeps down to the ha-ha, up to the moonamal tree and over the brow to Cinnamon Hill House; to the west a series of narrow terraces connect with the Field of Jars.

Opposite from top: A jack fruit; Looking from the carport towards the South Terrace

Left: Looking towards the Glass Bridge Pavilion. Below: Orchids

Lunuganga was conceived as a series of spaces to be moved through at leisure or occupied at certain times and for certain activities. Starting from the house it is possible to set out in any direction and combine the different parts of the garden into a variety of sequences. The whole can be taken in superficially by a brisk walker within half an hour, but there are enough surprises to amuse most people for days on end.

110　IV Lunuganga　　the south terrace　Above from top left: From Cinnamon Hill towards the house; The wall to Geoffrey Bawa's private bathroom court at the west end of the South Terrace; Roman bust in a niche in the wall of the South Terrace; Leaf patterns in concrete tables
Opposite: The South Terrace and the main entrance to the house

'The long view to the south ended with the temple, but in the middle distance was a ridge with a splendid ancient moonamal tree. When I placed a large Chinese jar under it, the hand of man was established in this middle distance. Now the eye stops here, travels to the glimmer of the lake beyond, to the slope across a long stretch of paddy fields and to the stupa on the crown of the far hill across the lake. In this view the vision of the lake was too slight and it became obvious that a part of the ridge needed to be lowered a few feet to establish the composition with a total finality. It now looks as if it has been there since the beginning of time.'

GEOFFREY BAWA, 1990

Pages 112–13: The view from the South Terrace towards Cinnamon Hill

Opposite from top: The West Verandah; Geoffrey Bawa's bathroom court

the main house Above from left: The reflecting pool outside Geoffrey Bawa's bedroom with doors opening to the West Verandah; Geoffrey Bawa's bedroom with his petrol-driven fan, painted doors by Laki Senanayake and a picture by Ivan Peries

the verandah room Above from left: Terracotta tiles by Donald Friend and Barbara Sansoni, set into a table; The main verandah at the north-west corner of the house – the original carport in 1948

IV Lunuganga

This page and opposite:
The twin frangipani trees on the North Terrace, planted by Geoffrey Bawa and carefully trained with weights

'In front of the house is a frangipani, which consists really of two trees whose trunks were twisted round each other, after which the branches were weighed down with big stones so that they stand almost horizontally and the leaves make a large flat parasol. When a family of peacocks settles on its branches it is like looking at a Chinese plate.'

GEOFFREY BAWA, date unknown

120 IV Lunuganga   north of the house   Above and opposite: The twin statues on the North Terrace

'The making of the garden evolved over a long time. The contours showed what the first moves must be. As the land was cleared, a wide and splendid view of the lake and the far shore started to emerge. One began to see the island in the lake – an island with the silhouette of a whale. The contours of the land being revealed, it now became obvious that a great deal of earth would have to be moved. Once the initial clearing of the land was done, the main views established themselves.'

GEOFFREY BAWA, 1990

'Looking back on the making of the garden, seeing it as it is now, it seems to me to be almost inevitable that it should be there. In my travels I had seen many splendid gardens and natural landscapes. I have always enjoyed visual pleasures and nature had often provided marvelous scenes and settings but human imagination had often emphasized this beauty. Water was important in any view – water and the play of light and shade gave me most pleasure – pleasure enhanced by a line of wall or a building – geometry and nature.' GEOFFREY BAWA, 1990

north of the house   Above: The edge of the North Terrace and the Cliff
Opposite: Looking down towards the Water Gardens
Pages 124–5: Looking across the Kitchen Terrace towards the door to the Glass Bridge Pavilion

'Rational building gives presence to both function and form, admits beauty and pleasure as well as purpose. These are my basic thoughts: thoughts on details; the proportion of rooms, doors and windows; the heights, the sweeps, the pitches of roofs; where one looks from a room, at what, and through what, at what is to be seen; how open or closed a view from a room should be.' GEOFFREY BAWA, date unknown

east of the house   Opposite: Looking back under the Glass Bridge Pavilion towards the entrance steps
Above: Inside the Glass Bridge Pavilion looking out towards the Sandela Pavilion

128 IV Lunuganga   east of the house   Above: The Eastern Terrace and the Hen House
Opposite from top: The flower of the cannonball tree; Indian nuga blossom; The Kitchen Verandah

'In my personal search I have been aware of the past – many periods of the past. There are so many instances when my eye was caught by a landscape with a small unimportant but beautiful building or a large and splendid one. The beauty of these buildings, gardens and landscapes leaves a considerable residue of subconscious understanding in the mind – a help to solve some present need: for the right placement of a building on site; for the need to frame and emphasise a view or to open or construct a space; a wish to get a definite degree of light or shade in a room.' GEOFFREY BAWA, date unknown

east of the house Above: Looking into the Sandela Pavilion
Opposite from top: The Sandela; Looking across the Eastern Terrace from the Sandela

Over the years, the original rubber trees were replaced by a variety of trees and shrubs. But this is not a garden of flower beds and gurgling fountains, of ordered parterres and pretty ponds; it is a civilized wilderness, a monochromatic composition of green on green, an ever-changing play of light and shade, a carefully orchestrated succession of hidden surprises and sudden views.

east of the house   Left: The edge of the Eastern Terrace

134　IV Lunaganga　　east of the house　　Above from left: The bay window of the Sandela; Within the Sandela

Left and opposite: Views of the Gothic Court, inspired by two windows given to Geoffrey Bawa by C. Anjalendran

east of the house   Opposite: Looking into the Gallery

Above from top: Looking from the Gallery into the Gothic Court; Sample silver flag made for the Kotte parliament; Kandyan wall bracket; Hindu deity on the Gallery Terrace

140 IV Lunuganga   east of the house   Above: The corner of the Eastern Terrace, a favourite spot for drinks
Opposite: Looking down from the Cliff towards the Black Pavilion Pool

IV Lunuganga 141

east of the house Above: Around the Black Pavilion Pool

Opposite: The Sundial in the Black Pavilion Pool

'Each part of the garden, inevitably an inseparable part of the whole, grew out of decisions that were not based on any prearranged formality: the garden planned itself, the shape of a tree or a shadow pointing the way. The long view to the south, ending at the temple on a far hill, initially emerged when the

east of the house

Above from top left: Rice paddy; The leopard at the Water Gate sculpted by Lidia Duchini; Looking across the rice paddy towards the Water Gate; Frangipani trees alongside the Broad Walk

Opposite: The Broad Walk looking towards the ruins of the Black Pavilion

thick jungle growth was cleared from the southern hill, while the wide northern view with the island established a scale to the whole composition – which later would contain so many smaller individual spaces, some open, some shaded, each different in feeling and mood.' GEOFFREY BAWA, 1990

east of the house   Opposite: Bamboosiana!

Above from top: View through the frangipani across the rice paddy; The Frangipani Avenue

Pages 148–9: View across the Black Pavilion Pool towards the Broad Walk

'Consult the Genius of the Place in all;

That tells the Waters or to rise or fall;

Or helps th' ambitious Hill the heav'ns to scale,

Or scoops in circling theatres the Vale ...'

ALEXANDER POPE, 1735

east of the house   Opposite and above: Around the Water Gardens

152　IV　Lunuganga　　east of the house　Above from top: Looking out from the Water Gate towards the island; The Water Gate
Opposite: The Water Gardens

Opposite from top: Steps up to the Western Terraces; The foot of the Western Terraces; The 'Pan Head'

Above from top: The Roman Pavilion; Bust of Geoffrey Bawa; An urn by Donald Friend beside the Roman Pavilion

Pages 156–7: Looking down from the Western Terraces – the two chairs were designed for the Kandalama Hotel

IV Lunuganga 155

west of the house Above: Details from around the well in the Field of Jars
Opposite: The Blue Pavilion

Discrete pavilions offer shade and space for contemplation, works of art are placed carefully to punctuate the pathways and link the vistas. Bacchanalian urns stare out from the undergrowth, a leopard lies in the dappled shade beside the lake, a marble youth points down from a parapet, and a grotesque Pan grins knowingly from the edge of the paddy.

Left: The bell near the Draftsmen's Pavilion

Opposite from top: The Draftsmen's Pavilion; A *Mal Lalli* (flower plank) screen dating from the visit of the Prince of Wales in 1875

IV Lunuganga

Opposite from top: The loggia beside the Bridge of Sighs; Details of the mural by Laki Senanayake; The tiled roof of the loggia

Above: Details of the mural by Laki Senanayake

IV Lunuganga 163

'For many years the garden had grown gradually into a place of many moods, the result of many imaginings, offering me a retreat to be alone or fellowfeel with friends. An added pleasure is one of seeing and feeling reactions to this place, from puzzlement to the silence of contentment, from the remarkable comment of a friend of a friend "This would be a lovely place to have a garden!" to the words of a lorry driver who walked round the garden whilst his bricks were being unloaded and said "But this is a very blessed place!"' GEOFFREY BAWA, 1990

west of the house Opposite: Looking from the Water Tower on Cinnamon Hill towards the southern slopes

Above: The top of Cinnamon Hill with the new moonamal tree (the original died soon after Geoffrey Bawa suffered his final stroke)

Pages 166–7: The wind pump on the southern slopes

Above: The loggia of Cinnamon Hill House;
Left: The terrace of Cinnamon Hill House – built in 1992, this was the last major addition to the garden

west of the house Above: Looking across the southern slopes towards the lake

Pages 170–71: Looking back across the ha-ha towards the house

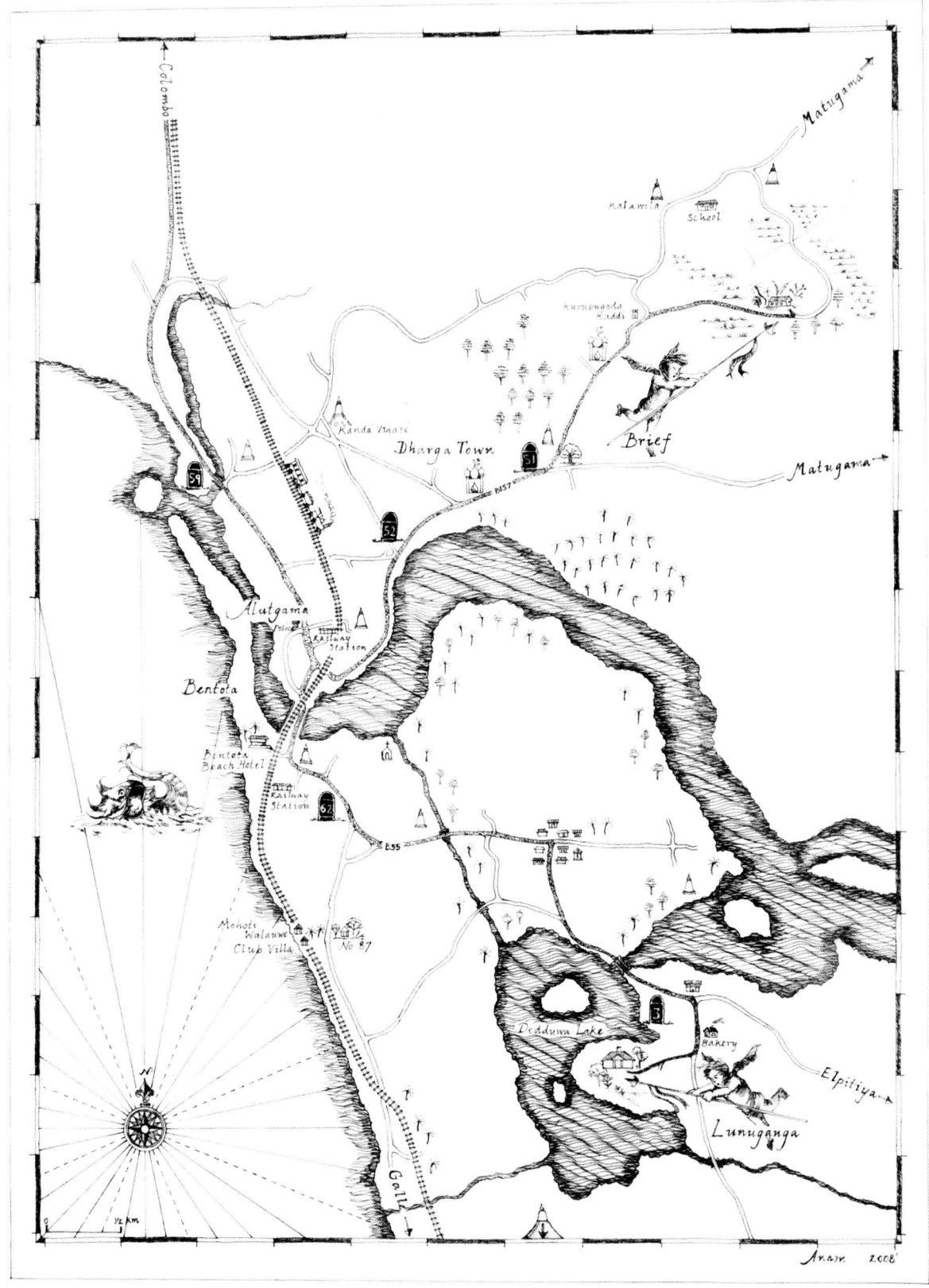

Visiting Brief

Brief Garden lies a few kilometres inland from the coastal town of Aluthgama. The route to Brief begins at a left fork at the southern end of the main street in Aluthgama and then follows the B.157 Mathugama road for 3 kilometres along the north bank of the Bentota River to Darga Town. Soon after the 51-kilometre post, a road on the left is marked by a Buddhist shrine and a Bo tree. This road leads after 1 kilometre to a small mosque from where a road forks to the right. This crosses a marsh and, after a further kilometre, climbs into some trees. A signpost announces Brief and points to a narrow road which crosses more marshland and skirts the side of a tree-clad hill. After 1 kilometre a small roundabout connects to a kabook road which doubles back up the hillside and through the woods to a tree-lined circus. Here a pair of bacchanalian gateposts reveal an avenue of sealing-wax palms. This leads finally to a second circus where a small door set in a samara-coloured wall serves as the main entrance to Brief.

Brief Garden is managed by Dooland de Silva and is open to visitors every day on payment of a modest entrance fee. Refreshments are available and lunch and dinner can be had by prior booking.

Telephone: +94 (0) 342 274462

Website: briefgarden.com

Visiting Lunuganga

Lunuganga lies about 60 kilometres south of Colombo and 3 kilometres inland from the resort town of Bentota. In Bentota, after crossing the bridge over the Bentota River, take the left turn a short distance beyond the 62-kilometre post and join the B.55 Elpitiya road. After 1.5 kilometres, follow the main road to the right and continue for 1 kilometre to the causeway over the neck of the Dedduwa Lake which offers a first view of Lunuganga across the water on the right. After 500 metres take the small road on the right and after a further 300 metres follow the narrow lane which forks right. This leads through woods and over a paddy field to the gates of Lunuganga.

Lunuganga is still managed and maintained by the non-profit Trust which Geoffrey Bawa established before his death. The gardens can be visited daily at 11 am, 2 pm and 3 pm. The Trust also operates a country hotel through a third party and food and refreshments are available.

The Ena de Silva House, built in Colombo by Geoffrey Bawa in 1960, was demolished in 2017 and rebuilt on the edge of the garden. It is open to the public.

Email: admin@geoffreybawa.com

Website: geoffreybawa.com

Opposite: 'How to reach Brief and Lunuganga', drawn by Anam Azeez for C. Anjalendran and based on Donald Friend's original map of Brief and Sumangala Jayatillaka's map of Lunuganga

Page 176: An urn in the Bathroom Garden at Brief

Glossary

Key
Sin. Sinhalese
Pali/San. Pali / Sanskrit

aralia tree *Sin.* frangipani tree (Lat. *Plumeria*)

arama *Pali/San.* a park monastery

aya *Sin.* a nurse

bodhigara *Pali/San.* a platform supporting a bo tree

bodhisattva *Pali/San.* one who is about to achieve buddhahood

bo tree *Sin.* peepul tree (Lat. *Ficus religiosa*)

bund the retaining structure of a reservoir

Burgher a person of mixed European and Sri Lankan descent

creeper an apprentice estate superintendent

dagoba *Sin.* a hemispherical relic mound

dewale *Sin.* a Hindu shrine frequented by Buddhists

Dutch Burgher a direct male-line descendant of a European employee of the Dutch East Indies Company

ganga *Sin.* river

guard-stone a carved stone placed beside an entrance

image house a building in a Buddhist temple which contains images of the Lord Buddha

kabook a soft laterite stone

moonamal tree *Sin.* (Lat. *Mimusops elengi*)

moon-stone a semi-circular carved stone placed on the ground at the entrance to a Buddhist temple

oya *Sin.* stream

pokuna *Sin.* pond

samara *Sin.* yellow-ochre-coloured paint applied to plaster walls

seema mallika *Sin.* an ordination platform for Buddhist monks

sri *Sin.* holy, hallowed, resplendent

stupa as for dagoba, a masonry hemisphere containing a Buddhist relic

tank a man-made reservoir

vihare *Sin.* temple

Bibliography

Bandaranayake, Senake. 'Among Asia's Earliest Surviving Gardens: The Royal and Monastic Gardens at Sigiriya and Anuradhapura', in Roland Silva, ed., *Historic Gardens and Sites*, ICOMOS, Colombo, 1993

Bawa, Bevis, *Briefly by Bevis*, Sapumal Foundation, Colombo, 1985

Bawa, Bevis, ed. Neville Weeraratne, *Bevis Bawa's Brief*, Brief Publications, 2011

Bawa, Geoffrey, Christoph Bon and Dominic Sansoni, *Lunuganga*, Times Editions, Singapore, 1990

De Silva, Shayari, ed., *Geoffrey Bawa: Drawing from the Archives*, Lars Müller, Zurich, 2023

Hetherington, Paul, *The Diaries of Donald Friend, Volume 3*, National Library of Australia, Canberra, 2005

—, *The Diaries of Donald Friend, Volume 4*, National Library of Australia, Canberra, 2006

Lewcock, Ronald, Barbara Sansoni and Laki Senanayake, *The Architecture of an Island*, Barefoot, Colombo, 1998

Macmillan, H. F., *Tropical Planting and Gardening with Special Reference to Ceylon*, Macmillan, London, 1956

Maugham, Robin, *Search for Nirvana*, Allen, London, 1975

Pope, Alexander, 'Epistle to Lord Burlington – On the Use of Riches', *Collected Poems*, Penguin, London, 1971

Robson, David, 'Lunuganga – The Story of a Garden', in Roland Silva, ed., *Historic Gardens and Sites*, ICOMOS, Colombo, 1993

—, *Bawa: The Complete Works*, Thames & Hudson, London, 2002

—, *Beyond Bawa: Modern Masterworks of Monsoon Asia*, Thames & Hudson, London, 2007

—, *The Architectural Heritage of Sri Lanka*, Talisman, Singapore, 2016

Robson, David and Sebastian Posingis, *In Search of Bawa*, Laurence King, London, 2016

—, *Bawa Staircases*, Laurence King, London, 2018

Taylor, Brian B., *Geoffrey Bawa*, Concept Media, Singapore, 1986; reprint Thames & Hudson, London, 1995

Wright, Arnold, *Twentieth Century Impressions of Ceylon*, Lloyd's, London, 1907

Credits

Key
T top, M middle, B bottom, L left, R right, C centre

Photographs
© Dominic Sansoni:
cover, 1, 2, 3, 7, 8, 10–11, 12TL/TR/BR, 13B, 14, 15, 16, 17BL/BR, 20, 21, 23, 24, 28, 29, 32, 35TR, 37MR, 40, 41, 42BL/BR, 43TR, 44, 46LM/LB, 47, 50–91, 92, 94, 96, 97B, 99T/BL, 102–71, 176
courtesy of Tea Trails Ltd: 28, 29BL/BR
courtesy of Dooland de Silva: 32, 35TR, 37MR, 41T, 42BR, 43TR, 44;
courtesy of Cedric de Silva: 47
courtesy of the Lunuganga Trust: 94, 96, 99T
courtesy of Barbara Sansoni: 42BL
courtesy of Sapumal Foundation: 41B
courtesy of Rachel Sutherland: 46LM, 99T

© David Robson:
end papers, 12BL, 13TL/TR, 17T, 18, 19, 22, 25, 26, 30, 33, 34, 35BL, 36, 37BL/TR, 38, 39BL/TR/MR, 42TL, 43UMR/LMR/BR, 48–9, 95, 98, 99BR, 101, 172
courtesy of Kandy House Hotel: 30
from the Bawa Archive: 33BL, 34, 35BL, 36, 37BL/TR, 38, 39
courtesy of the Lunuganga Trust: 98, 101
courtesy of C. Anjalendran: end papers, 43UMR/LMR/BR, 46LB, 48–9, 172

© Christoph Bon: 97TM/M, 100BL

© from the collection of Palinda de Silva: 27TR/MR/BR, 31

© from the collection of Ismeth Raheem: 27BL

Illustrations
With the permission of the Art Gallery of New South Wales and the Estate of Donald Friend: 45RT
With the permission of the National Library of Australia and the Estate of Donald Friend: 46LT
With the permission of Ken & Swyrie Balendra: 45MR

Other sources
Extracts and illustrations from the unpublished memoirs of Bevis Bawa, the Brief Visitors' Book and the poem 'The Bawa of Brief' are reproduced with the permission of Dooland de Silva and the Estate of Bevis Bawa.
Extracts from the Lunuganga Visitors' Book are reproduced with the permission of the Lunuganga Trust.
Extracts from the Diaries of Donald Friend are reproduced with permission of the National Library of Australia and the estate of Donald Friend.